THROUGH THE EYE OF THE NEEDLE

Through the Eye
of the Needle

Bill Speidel

Edited by Linda Lewis
Illustrated by Gus Swanberg
Cover Illustration by Frank Renlie

ISBN 0-914890-04-2

TABLE OF CONTENTS

Foreword

A LONG TIME AGO Bill Speidel told me: "There are a certain number of people in this town who get things done, who know what's important and what's going on. The rest we just keep around for bulk."

That is vintage Speidel, the man you are going to meet in this book. When Bill Talked about who managed to "get things done" in Seattle, he was not referring exclusively to the power hitters of finance, the wheeler-dealers, the bombardiers of the Chamber of Commerce.

He knew all about that kind. In his lifetime, he worked for and against many of the genre. He wrote about them in his books. Some he liked, some he tolerated, and some he merely ignored. But he was never overwhelmed by any of them; quite a few, he believed, we just have around for bulk.

The people Bill Speidel liked most were those in whose veins flowed the rich juices of humanity. If they were a little off-center, that was all right too. He admired the late Ivar Haglund, for example, and Ivar had abundant affection for Bill.

Mere generosity was not enough for Bill, who spent most of his life in Seattle examining and writing about the native species. He liked people with flair, masters of the difficult art of being fully alive. He relished people with ideas. His own idea of pleasure was a long conversation with such Seattle wits and sages as Guy Williams, Jim Faber, Bob Ward, Ralph Anderson, Dick White, Nancy Davis, Vic Steinbrueck and, of course, Ivar.

"I love people with ideas, I mean people to whom ideas are important," he once said. It is not generally known that Bill actually paid a man, one whom Bill judged the best idea man in town, to hang around his office. The pay was good ($10 an hour), there was no heavy lifting, and all the idea merchant had to do was sit down and talk off the top of his head for a while.

Bill loved stories, especially anecdotes that illustrated a point. His books were always rich with local anecdotes—he wrote a half-dozen such books in his lifetime. His first book, "You Can't Eat Mt. Rainier," published in the early 1950s, was really an effort to promote fine dining in the Northwest. If you happen to have a copy of "You Can't Eat Mt. Rainier," I suggest you cherish it. It has become a collector's item over the years.

The man so many people called "Spy" also wrote such lively books as "The Wet Side of the Mountains," "You Still Can't Eat Mt. Rainier," "Sons of the Profits" and "Doc Maynard." All of them were stories about Seattle figures, stories that Speidel cherished—and this last book, completed before Bill's death about a year ago, is no exception.

The Bill Speidel I knew was a man or humor, courtliness, grace and good manners. As I remember him as a young man, Bill had close-cropped hair, a voice that dominated any room he was in, and a strong-jawed masculine good looks. The voice. I would get to know that voice during dozens of chance meetings, over drinks and lunch, and through hundreds of telephone calls.

As a youngster out of high school I first glimpsed Bill Speidel under rather odd circumstances. He was a reporter on the *Seattle Times,* his first newspaper job, and for reasons that escape memory I happened to be in the *Times* city room, awaiting the pleasure of another reporter.

As it happened, this reporter got into a discussion with another scribe (I remember being extravagantly impressed) and they talked about a story one of them was doing on a prominent public official. The official had announced his intention to marry his paramour and I remember one reporter saying, with a chuckle, "What's he want to marry her for? He's getting all . . ."

"Gentlemen! Gennntulmen!" came the strong voice from a nearby desk. The tone was bemused, yet slightly indignant. It was a half-amused rebuke that he should be forced to overhear such unseemly chatter. I still have that wonderful picture of Bill Speidel to this day.

Later I got to know Bill Speidel when I worked as a rookie sports-writer on the old *Seattle Star*. He then wrote a news-feature column that the *Star* played on its front page. He would come in rather late at night, the hours I worked, and there would be only two of us, separated by a couple of desks.

I remember thinking, at first, that Bill was standoffish. He rarely spoke or engaged in any kind of shop talk. It was only later that I realized Bill Speidel was a serious man when confronted by a type-writer; faced with the important job of turning out readable, informa-tive copy, he had no time for small talk. I consider it my extreme good fortune that our friendship developed over the ensuing years into the kind of easy camaraderie that one remembers with warmth and affec-tion.

It should be noted—in fact, emphasized—that few of Seattle's establishment figures, the ones Bill wrote about, contributed as much to this city as Bill did himself. He played many roles in Seattle.

He was, foremost, a preservationist, whose greatest gift, probably, was his devotion to restoring and enhancing Pioneer Square. He would be the last to take full credit for it, but he was a central figure in saving this wonderful, historic part of Seattle.

Yes, he was many things during his life as a quintessential Seattle-ite—preservationist, publicist, writer, historian, businessman, political operator, adman, publisher and public speaker. All of these activities gave him the necessary skeptical insight to write well of the city he loved. But they also gave him the ability to go out on the firing lines to lobby in person for what he believed would make Seattle a better place in which to live.

As a political operative, he mostly worked in Republican causes and for Republican candidates, but I firmly believe he was a populist by temperament. For example, he always carried with him a few quarters. These he passed out almost ritually to the bums and winos who were being pushed around by the gentrification he had wrought in Pioneer Square. He made no big thing of it. All he said was, "We need these people for color. When they're gone, what do we do—call Actor's Equity?"

June Almquist, assistant managing editor in charge of administration for the *Seattle Times,* was an early cohort of Bill Speidel's. She worked as Bill's "Girl Friday," a now obsolete job description. When June told a friend, back in 1946, that she had a chance to work in Bill's ad agency, he told her, "After working for him about a year, you'll be able to write a book called 'Life in a Squirrel Cage.'" That was very nearly no exaggeration.

In the beginning, times were tough and clients infrequent. "But when it came time to divide up the money to see who got paid each month, Bill always set aside enough for my salary."

Later, in a two-part profile of Bill, June wrote of her three years with this man who would later become a Seattle institution:

"I was his only staff. Our office was a cubby hole on the second floor of the downtown Y.M.C.A. (The Y.M. was one of Speidel's accounts, and paid him by giving office space and facilities for $50 a month.) The room was just big enough to hold two desks, three chairs and a filing cabinet . . .

"To say we operated hand-to-mouth in those days is absolute fact. In order to have something in hand to put into the mouth, Spy took on just about any publicity account that came along. Just so it wasn't something crooked was the only criteria."

For 20 years he operated the agency. Along the way he bought Seattle Guide, Inc., a weekly entertainment-tourist guide, then he established Nettle Creek Publishing Co. to publish his books. Believe it, he owned his own books; when necessary, he borrowed the money to put them out—and they were written in his own style, saying what he wanted to say. No nonsense from second-party editors and publishers.

All of his books sold well, in excess of 10,000 copies, a handsome figure for a regional book. The early Bill Speidel that I knew, the handsome guy with the close-cropped hair, the strong voice, the square jaw—he was too much of a skeptical reporter to her-worship the Seattle pioneers he wrote about.

In his own bemused, humorous way, Bill once told me that shared greed had much to do with the building of Seattle. "If you want to find out what really happened," he said, "follow the money." It was no accident that Bill titled one of his more successful books "Sons of the Profits." A short quotation illustrates Bill's skeptical view of the people we later named streets after.

"That they built a city in the process was purely coincidental," Bill wrote of Seattle's pioneers. "If they could have made more money by not building a city, then that is what they would have done . . .

"They regarded the Indians, the Legislature, the federal government, the competing towns on the Sound, their fellow businessmen down the street, the mud, trees, hills, and Northern Pacific Railroad and the hop house of the 1890s as necessary evils that must be coped with.

"Their brand of coping presumed that the end justified the means."

Back in the 1960s, I was writing a kind of three-dot gossip column for the *Seattle Post-Intelligencer,* one that depended heavily on other people for information. To this day, I am grateful for Bill Speidel and his sharp eye for the offbeat, the humorous, the ironical. He had a newsman's nose.

During one period I noticed that Spy was phoning in a sizeable number of items about Alcoholics Anonymous. At first I thought he had befriended some ex-alcoholic, who gave him notes and quotes. I should have known. Later I learned that at exactly 10 a.m., November 24, 1964, Bill Speidel took his last drink. My old drinking buddy had given the game back to the boys.

He made no secret of this, for in some things Speidel could be breathtakingly candid. He remained "dry" until the end of his life, at 76, on May 4, 1988, and here again, typically Speidel, he did what he could to promote the work of Alcoholics Anonymous. It should not even be thought of as a paradox, I suppose, that Bill's only real "hero" among Seattle's pioneers was the generous, garrulous, tippling "Doc" Maynard. Bill devoted an entire book to Doc. He also bought a tavern in Pioneer Square and renamed it "Doc Maynard's."

Late in life, Bill became a multi-faceted businessman. Rehabilitated Pioneer Square, with which he had so much to do, grew from a run-down Skid Road into a fashionable, upscale neighborhood of boutiques, bookstores, restaurants, specialty shops, and luxury apartments. Much of the Square's success came because of another Speidel idea—making a tourist attraction of the "other," underground Seattle that existed before the Great Fire of 1889. In 1965, Bill established the Underground Tours that now see 120,00 people a year go through—a visitor attraction second only to the Space Needle itself.

So many stories about bill have that "typical" stamp on them. One of these concerns his later success with the *Seattle Guide.* By now, of course, the *Guide* is a flourishing Seattle institution and was, for many years, edited by Lou Dewey.

The day after Bill's death, I called Lou Dewey to confirm a story I'd heard about the *Guide.* Was it true, I asked her, that a large company had once tried to buy the *Guide* from Speidel at a price that would have netted a sizeable amount of money to Bill? He told them to make their buyout presentation to the *Guide's* employees.

They made their presentation and the employees voted not to sell. "Then that's it," Speidel told the would-be buyers. "The *Guide* is not for sale."

I know that as you read the pages of this final Speidel book, something of his spirit, his warmth, his friendship will rub off on you. One gropes for some concluding words of tribute, but it was Lou Dewey who delivered, I think, the shortest, most eloquent tribute to this man who had such a great impact on Seattle.

"The guy was wonderful," she said. "We're losing too many giants in this city. The kind that count, not the developers and bankers. I tell you, the guy was wonderful."

Emmett Watson

Dedication

Bill's proudest life achievement was marrying Shirley. This book is dedicated to Shirley Speidel.

Hourglass Figure

Pie in the Sky

WENTY-FIVE YEARS AGO, when I was a lot newer to the history business, I wrote a book that started out: "It is virtually illegal to write a story about Seattle that does not include a four-color picture of sailboats on Lake Washington with the Floating Bridge and Mount Rainier in the background."

But that isn't Seattle. Just the setting.

Since that time, I've picked up a lot more knowledge and a few more adjectives and can start this book by saying: It is illegal, immoral, unconstitutional and fattening to take a picture of Seattle that does not include the Space Needle.

The Needle comes closer to being the essence of Seattle than anything we have tried in our fourteen decades. It stands for the risk-takers who have made us what we are—a regal city, built on luck, location and lunacy.

For a long time we used Mount Rainier as our symbol. This was distressing to people in Tacoma, who've always had the mistaken belief that you can get something for nothing and who are trying still to get the mountain named after their town.

Years ago the editor of the Seattle weekly *Argus* put it like this: "Will some kindly disposed persons tell me, if they can, why the inspired

Eddie Carlson

idiots of Tacoma insist on calling the beautiful mountain after their dinky little city?"

Neither city has any real claim to Mount Rainier, because it was the Lord God Almighty who provided us with that natural resource.

The Space Needle, on the other hand . . . Aha!

It contains all of the elements that make up the Seattle spirit.

Seattle has a high proportion of people who will try almost anything . . . which is why we are number one in the nation with bankruptcies.

A Lofty Idea

The Space Needle was a highly (607 feet) chancy project. It came to life in the mind of one Edward E. Carlson while he was dining in the restaurant at the top of the Stuttgart (West Germany) Tower. He and all the other diners had paid a dollar for the privilege of riding up 663 feet and ordering meals. Eddie was intrigued. On his napkin, he doodled restaurants in the sky.

That was in 1959 when Eddie was chairman of the state of Washington's World's Fair Committee. The fair was scheduled to be a main attraction of 1962. Whether it would even occur was questionable in 1959.

The fair lacked a galvanizing symbol. And it needed financing.

Eddie, gifted and bright, was one of the more enterprising hotel men in Seattle, thought of how the federal coffers were beginning to open up to anything that even sounded like space. The Russians had beaten the United States to the punch by launching Sputnik.

It doesn't really much matter whether he had read Robert Browning's quote about a man's reach needing to exceed his grasp—although Eddie did attend the University of Washington.

If Eddie had been employed by some government agency, he would have chomped away at his high-rise dinner and gone back to his hotel for a good night's sleep. But chance is the golden opportunity of the trained mind. And Eddie couldn't sleep.

Those people in that restaurant had paid a buck a head for the privilege of riding to the top of the tower and then buying dinner.

The federal government was throwing money at space.

The upcoming world's fair, dubbed the Century 21 Exposition, needed a symbol.

It all combined to look like pie in the sky to Eddie.

"Oh God! Pass the Aspirin"

The response of those back home who were trying to cope with the scramble that was supposed to coalesce into the fair practically "the day after tomorrow," was "Oh God!" followed by three extra-strength aspirins.

Eddie knew he needed someone to tell him that he wasn't proposing the silliest thing anyone ever imagined.

He had lunch with Jim Douglas, the exposition's vice president in charge of construction.

Douglas suggested they go together to see architect John Graham, who was building a revolving restaurant in Honolulu.

And that's when the fun began.

First, because you've got to have some place to put the damned thing.

The land for the world's fair had been acquired by condemnation. And with attorney Al Schweppe waiting in the wings to challenge illegalities, there was no way any of that land could be turned over to a private enterprise operation.

Nobody had put his money where his mouth was, and the don'ters were having their day.

It is my long-held opinion that Seattle is made up of doers, don'ters, doubters and deadheads. The doers get things done because the don'ters try to stop them. The doubters stick around to see them fall flat on their faces. And the deadheads never know anything's happening, but we need them to buy the tickets.

Taking the Bait

Faced with the impossibility of building a tower on the world's fair site, Seattle's doers rose like rainbow trout going for a Royal Coachman fly.

Bagley Wright, one of the newcomers to town who makes things happen, saw a rendering of the Needle on the wall in John Graham's office. He asked what it was.

"Something that probably will never happen," was the architect's dour reply.

At that point, the proposed sculpture had been turned down by federal, state, county and city bureaucrats of the kind who never do anything unless it has been done 99 and $44/100$th times before.

David E. "Ned" Skinner, a native son, and Wright chartered a helicopter and took it to 1,000 feet above the grounds of the Century 21 Exposition.

"We could sell tickets at a buck a head for the view at this height!" Skinner shouted.

"We couldn't build a structure this high for that kind of money!" Wright screamed back.

So the pilot obligingly began lowering the craft. And at 607 feet, the economic and the aesthetic lines converged.

The elevation of the Needle was born . . . but not the exact location.

The only room for private enterprise on the exposition grounds was owned by the Shrine, which had notions of a big addition to its crippled children's program. All of the other possible sites in the vicinity were owned by people looking for big cash and early retirement.

Then the fellows learned why it is better to be lucky than smart.

The city of Seattle owned a tiny hunk of ground, fifty feet square, and was willing to sell at a reasonable price. The city council agreed to $60,000 for the parcel.

Tough on the Shrine crippled children's program and the property owners elsewhere who believed that a comfortable cash position was better than a clear conscience.

But it was surely good for the symbol of our city.

The cost of the sculpture was going to be about two million dollars.

That was fine until some building inspector thought it should be earthquake-proof.

The cost rose to four million.

"Well," said Wright to Skinner. "We can dig up another two million or . . ."

"What's the other choice?"

"Leave town."

The Sound of One Clapp Handling

In 1962, four million bucks was worth four million bucks. So they went to Norton Clapp.

"I was working for Weyerhaeuser at the time," Clapp explained. (And so he was, as chairman of the board.) "You remember our friend Al Link, my 'no' man? Well, I turned them over to Al. A little while later, I said to Al, 'Whatever happened to that deal?' He said: 'We're in for a million.'"

Everybody agrees that the deal would not have gone through if it had not been for the Bank of California. Wright, Skinner, Clapp, Graham and contractor Howard Wright formed the Pentagram Corporation and agreed to lend their credit. But nobody wanted anybody else to see his net worth statement, and the bank wouldn't make the loan without it.

Tom McQuaid ran the bank locally.

"Don't you guys unroll those plans in my office!" McQuaid screamed.

"How tall is this building?" the boss in San Francisco asked.

"Sixty stories," McQuaid said.

"How many rooms does it have?"

"Two."

A short silence. Then:

"Tom, I want to tell you a little story.

"I got into the banking business in the Midwest by making a loan to a circus which had only a herd of elephants as collateral. If I'm forced out of the banking business now by making a loan on a crazy scheme like your Space Needle, it won't be any wilder than that loan on the herd of elephants."

Then Eddie Carlson got a call from Al Link, who said: "On that Space Needle thing of yours . . . Norton and Ned Skinner and Bagley and Howie Wright and John Graham are going to put up the money. Would you run the restaurant?" ("You" being Western Hotels, now Westin Hotels and Resorts.)

Eddie said: "Sure. Easy."

Needling the Doubters

Ewen Dingwall, fair manager, estimates that the importance of that action was beyond calculation with regard to staging the fair. It broke the logjam.

Less than a year before the fair opened, many of the doubters were still at it. As the Needle climbed higher into the sky, it became a thermometer of civic enthusiasm for the fair. People looked up and actually saw the pie in the sky . . .

And it was orbiting.

The Needle became the thematic symbol around which everything else revolved. Promoters had their visual. The Needle was on the cover of Life twice. It was on a first-class (then four-cent) stamp. A milling company created a Space Noodle.

The final design of the sculpture is something a guy could end up in a lawsuit about, but it was either John Graham's, whose architectural firm handled the matter, or Victor Steinbrueck's, who took the trouble of calling me from his deathbed to make sure I didn't credit Graham.

Graham's designer Art Edwards sketched the first concepts.

Steinbrueck introduced the hour-glass figure and designed the final tripod legs.

A Perfect Wasp-waisted Reflection

The Needle's shape reflects us perfectly. The land in between Seattle Center and Pioneer Square, squeezed by Puget Sound on one side and Lake Washington on the other, is the city with the hour-glass figure.

Nobody building it knew the Needle would become the worldwide symbol of our city.

The Pentagram enterprisers, being good business people, refrained from covering the structural steel with concrete so if it failed they could sell it for salvage and recoup a couple of bucks.

Then more than two million people showed up at the fair, and the Needle was here to stay.

We know now that the Needle marks the geographic center of the United States. You doubt that? Just take some string and a globe of the world. Okay. Measure the distance from Seattle to Portland, Maine; then from Seattle to New York City; then to Miami, Florida; then to Laredo, Texas; to Honolulu, and, finally, to Point Barrow, Alaska. Now divide by six. You'll find that the Space Needle is equidistant from the farthest points in the United States.

Another thing to note about its location is that the Needle's center of gravity is under land that originally belonged to Seattle's first builder. Louisa Boren Denny initiated construction of the first permanent structure in what would become Seattle.

The spark she lit under the men who came to Seattle with her is generally overlooked in our history books. Our historians have tended to confine themselves to the deeds of the men only. We'll go part of the way toward telling the other half of the story in these pages.

Luck, Location and Lunacy

When we look at Seattle's history through the eye of the Needle, we see a tale of luck, location and lunacy. We see the story of people believing in the time-honored adage: "Make no small plans."

Beginning with the arrival of our founder, Dr. D. S. Maynard, in the fall of 1850, we have had more people willing to take more chances than the rest of 'em.

It's the kind of chain reaction that feeds upon itself and is as active today as it was fourteen decades ago.

Edwin Ferry Johnson was the first to predict that a location on Puget Sound would become the Queen City of the Pacific. Johnson was the leading railroader of his day, the author of the first book to propose construction of a railroad across the United States to the Pacific Coast.

Johnson's day was the early 1850s, when the rage for laying out towns in the Pacific Northwest reached its zenith. It was a time when the future of railroading seemed boundless.

Railways had proved to be the most efficient method of hauling things and people over land, and the tracks could go practically anywhere. Along with the railroad boom came the realization that because of the great circle of the earth, some place on Puget Sound would be the shortest distance in the U.S. between New York and the "riches of the Orient."

And that's when David Swinson Maynard, equipped with the know-how of city building—garnered from eighteen years of doing just that in Cleveland, Ohio—came to Seattle.

The Trail to Seattle

*I*T HAD BEEN NINE YEARS since D. S. Maynard found his wife in bed with another guy. He had gone through two or three fortunes in and around Cleveland. He happened at that moment to be in a position to leave his wife with a home that was free and clear and a "sufficient competence" to feed herself and their kids.

And so, with no love lost between the principals, Maynard "took the cars to Sandusky" and embarked west from there.

That was on April 9, 1850.

Doc Maynard joined a wagon train that was supposed to take him to the well-financed political campaign of John B. Weller in California. He had run one campaign for Weller in Ohio, but the results sent the candidate west for the Gold Rush rather than to the governor's mansion.

After making a killing during Forty-niner days, Weller decided he would like to be the first U.S. Senator from California. The Ohio race had been close enough for Weller to want Doc Maynard to give the campaign game another try.

The seed for the city of Seattle was germinated in the mud of the Oregon Trail.

A cholera epidemic had killed 20,000 people on that 2,000-mile trail.

For the most part, wolves were God's morticians.

If crosses had been raised above all of those whom cholera claimed, the Oregon Trail would have "resembled a broken picket fence," as one health authority put it.

The world did not know what caused this awful plague, and there was a considerable body of religious opinion that it was God visiting His wrath upon sinners. But there was one thing we did know, and that was that anyone insane enough to touch the dead and dying was almost certainly at 100 percent risk.

About eighty-five miles west of Fort Kearney in Nebraska, the path of Doc Maynard's wagon train bound for California came upon the path of a woman in a wagon train bound for the Pacific Northwest. And it was under these conditions and at this place that the man and woman who became the father and mother of Seattle met and ignored the wrath of God.

Doc Maynard persisted in rendering aid to the sick and dying. One of those he tended was a recently widowed woman named Catherine Broshears, who, according to the entry in the doctor's diary, was "ill in mind and body" and refused to leave her dead and dying to the ravages of wolves.

What he did not mention in his diary was that this was a case of love at first sight. Nothing he had done in the past or would do in the future would be more important than being with this woman.

Sounds pretty dramatic, doesn't it?

But under the circumstances, a little drama is not excessive.

So their separate paths became one.

And they headed for a mutual destiny . . .

Which they would call the city of Seattle . . .

Treating the sick and dying en route.

To complicate their lives, Catherine's jealous sister, Susanna, got a gun and tried to kill the doctor. And if that wasn't enough, the "easy does it" doc had failed to have his long-since deceased marriage in Cleveland declared legally dead.

Nevertheless, Maynard rerouted his trip to California to escort the young widow to Olympia, to the home of her brother, Michael T. Simmons, who would spend a mighty effort trying to find his sister a partner other than the doctor.

First, the Location

On October 9, 1850, Doc Maynard took off for an exploration of the land between the Columbia River and the Strait of Juan de Fuca. He was looking for a spot to put a town.

He met up with Isaac N. Ebey, who had preceded him through the same country looking for a farm.

They agreed that Elliott Bay was the spot. It was the nearest good anchorage to the lowest pass in the Cascades.

The piece of land we now call Pioneer Square, the "birthplace of Seattle," was the logical place for the town. The main channel of the Duwamish River followed the shoreline of Beacon Hill as far north as King Street where it turned west to what we now call Alaskan Way where it turned north and gouged out a deep channel for about 800 yards.

Maynard had his location, but he had three problems that he was aware of: He had no money. He had no legal right to marry the young widow. And he needed at least to visit Weller, the man whose political activities had drawn him west.

He had a fourth problem that he didn't know about.

A group of young innocents had just loaded up a wagon train and started west from Illinois.

The Denny men would eventually decide to do their farming on Puget Sound instead of in Oregon's valley of the Willamette. David Denny would have the foresight to declare "room for a thousand families in the Duwamish Valley."

While the Denny party was coming west, Doc Maynard spent a year cutting and splitting by hand 400 cords of wood, which he took to San Francisco and sold for $16,000.

He persuaded the Oregon Territorial Legislature to grant him a divorce. Catherine persuaded her brother that she would to marry the doctor or no one at all.

When he returned to his town site in late March of 1852, having won the hand of the fair maiden . . .

He found the ground he wanted down by the river staked out.

The Denny party had driven its stakes between the spots where the Space Needle and the Kingdome stand today.

And promptly retired to their cabins at Alki Point . . .

For a very simple reason . . .

Their leader didn't know what to do next.

Louisa Boren

Honesty and past neglect compel me to add Louisa Boren to the credits here. Not only did she know what to do next; she did it.

She laid the foundations for the first building in what would become the city of Seattle.

Louisa had a lot of spunk and would have continued to build the city before Doc Maynard showed up. But the vacillating Arthur Denny, leader of the party, saw to it that she was physically restrained.

There was no love lost between those two . . .

Not then . . .

Not ever.

When it came time for Doc Maynard to come back and put his town together, there it was—preempted.

Then the Luck

That's when the doctor found out it's better to be lucky than smart.

He was called upon to treat the malaria-ridden Arthur Denny at Alki Point.

In those days, the drug commonly administered against malaria was laudanum, which is opium dissolved in alcohol.

Arthur Denny was a teetotaler.

The alcohol alone would have made him reel.

With opium in it . . .

Well . . .

On a lovely opium jag then, Denny gave Maynard that "worthless" piece of swamp down by the mouth of the river. Maynard claimed he would use it for a fishing camp.

When Denny sobered up, he found he had given away what would become the most valuable piece of property west of Chicago and north of San Francisco.

Maynard's fishing village turned out to be fifty-eight square blocks, including thirty acres for a university and the land routed by the federal government as the terminus of a transcontinental railroad.

Before he was through, he had negotiated with the Indians a treaty for 58,000 acres, approximately the size of the city of Seattle.

The campaign to create the Queen City of the Pacific was under way.

Maynard's vision helped establish the city's "make no small plans" reputation.

And it marked the beginning of history through the eye of the Needle.

Maynard and Denny Street Layout

Ooooo, Louisa

T HE FIRST REASON for considering the Space Needle as the essence of our city comes from the fact that its center of gravity lies beneath the donation claim of Louisa Boren and David T. Denny. And because of some kind of celestial osmosis, it has soaked up the spirit of those two people.

You don't get or keep a great city without you got somebody willing to be on a first-name basis with risk. Sometimes the risk-takers win and sometimes they lose, but that really isn't the important part. The important part lies in the fact that they knew they were taking a chance at the time, and they knew the odds against them, but they were willing to go ahead anyway.

Louisa Boren and David T. Denny were among Seattle's first real risk-takers.

Let me hasten to explain that David and Louisa were husband and wife, a condition which in their day required that she assume his last name. That small detail, of course, didn't change their personalities. She was the stronger and, I suspect, the brighter of the two. She was older than he by nearly five years. In a previous book I made the facetious remark that she wet-nursed him until he was of age, and then she married him. That may or may not have been the truth. But it certainly is not of any consequence. They were a great pair of human beings who got along together, which made for a fine contribution to our city.

The one point of friction between them was David's older brother Arthur.

David worshipped him.

Louisa hated him.

I have been inclined to share Louisa's opinion of her brother-in-law, chiefly on the grounds that he was the first one in our history to want a free ride and get one. He was another one of those born with the philosophy that a comfortable cash position is better than a clear conscience.

The Denny family had loaded four wagons for the trip west from Cherry Grove, Illinois. Louisa asked permission to take along her favorite mirror. The answer was no. She hid it in a wagon.

She realized Christmas would come no matter where they were, so she hid presents for the children, too. No one else in the party thought to do that.

Louisa's vigilance saved the Denny party at least a couple of times on the trip west. She sounded the alarm when some drunken boatmen would have allowed their craft to go over the falls at The Dalles, Oregon. And when one of the younger kids, sleeping on the bank of the Columbia, rolled out of her blankets and headed for the river, it was Louisa to the rescue.

Family unity hit the final rock of dissension in Portland when Arthur and David disagreed with their father John over the destination of the trip. Up to that point, all had thought they would settle in the Willamette Valley and farm.

Reports of a place called Puget Sound appealed to Arthur. He wanted to go the extra miles north. David sided with him and against their father. Arthur sent David north to assess the lay of the land. David arrived in Elliott Bay on September 18, 1851, and sent word to Arthur, who was down with malaria in Portland, that there was room for a thousand families to farm in the Duwamish Valley.

Arthur arrived on November 13, 1851.

Our history textbooks list Arthur's arrival as the date on which our city was founded.

The encyclopedias list February 15, 1852, as the actual founding date because that was the day on which three claims of 320 acres each were staked between today's Space Needle and Kingdome, ground which would be the city of Seattle.

Arthur had led David, his brother-in-law Carson D. Boren and another member of the party, William N. Bell, in a canoe around Elliott Bay. Arthur tested the depth of the water with horseshoes tied to a clothesline. When he found a good sheltered harbor close to timber, he didn't waste any time staking his waterfront claim. Neither did his two paddling buddies. (David was not old enough to stake a claim.)

Arthur is known as the father of our city.

But then he wrote the first history book, and I suppose anyone is entitled to be the hero of his own book.

On the other hand, the men who staked those claims quickly retired to their original settlement at Alki Point, wondering what to do next...

And stayed there for the next forty-five days...

Until Doc Maynard arrived on March 31 and moved everybody across the bay.

An April Fool's Founding

There is some disputation on this. But it gives me pleasure to think that our city was founded on April Fool's Day.

Meanwhile, the spunky Louisa got sick to death of the inactivity at Alki and, with another woman, paddled across the bay and started building the first cabin in what eventually became the city of Seattle.

There's a brass marker at the corner of Second and Cherry where she started the whole thing. The only problem with the marker, imbedded in the Hoge Building, is that it gives the credit to Louisa's brother. It cites Carson D. Boren as having built the first cabin home in Seattle in April of 1852.

Carson may have finished the job. But only because Louisa had the gumption to start it.

When she got home after her first day of construction, Louisa met with some mighty upset and embarrassed men. They got up off their duffs long enough to physically restrain her from going back across the bay for another day of building.

Louisa's efforts at turning the frontier into home did not stop just because the menfolk thwarted one project. She had brought some sweetbrier seeds along on her trip west. She was able to plant them without ruffling the men's feelings.

Cultivation rather than construction is what Louisa is known for, if

17

she gets any credit at all in our history books. She has come down to us as the "Sweetbrier Bride."

She and David finally moved into a cabin on their donation claim in the northern end of the new city. She planted sweetbrier all around it. Sweetbrier was still growing in the area more than a hundred years later when the Space Needle was planted there.

The Big Blooper

THE GREATEST BLOOPER in Seattle history was committed on May 23, 1853. That's the day that Arthur Denny and Doc Maynard filed plats of their claims.

That's the day Seattle's streets were permanently screwed up.

The streets of Seattle should have been laid out north to south and east to west, as they are between King Street and Yesler Way, in the area that was Doc Maynard's original claim. However, between Yesler and the Space Needle, the streets run northwest to southeast. This irrevocable dislocation came about because Arthur Denny refused to believe that Doc Maynard could be right about anything.

Not only that...

For years Arthur Denny got away with blaming Doc Maynard for the mistake. The teetotaling Arthur fixed the tippling Doc with responsibility for the severe case of the bends in our streets. Arthur's version of the story had Doc Maynard too "stimulated" to see straight when he submitted his plat.

Clarence Bagley, dean of Seattle historians, knew about the mistake and the misplaced blame but let Denny's story stand in his first history of Seattle published in 1916.

But Bagley's knowledge bugged him for the next thirteen years, and when he rewrote the history in 1929, he had to come out with it and this is what he said:

> *On the twenty-third of May, 1853, two plats were filed with the county auditor adjoining each other and alike in the width of the streets and size of lots and blocks, but not in agreement in the directions in which the streets aimed; north and south streets instead of being continuous in alignment made offsets where the two plats joined.*
>
> *Denny used his survey of his and Boren's land as a base line and laid north and south streets parallel with it and intersecting streets at right angles; those streets taking the hills the steepest way.*
>
> *Maynard insisted on making the direction of the streets conform to the points of the compass.*
>
> *If all of the early plats had, like Maynard's, been made to conform to the cardinal points with some minor adjustments, the present city grades would be more serviceable and property owners would have been saved the expense of many subsequent regrades and condemnations of property to be used for street purposes.*
>
> *First Avenue would have been extended by an easy grade through the university tract, with contiguous streets conforming to it.*

Arthur Denny was not the kind of guy who forgave easily. Especially not the fellow who doped him into giving away the central business district of his city. From that hazy day on, Arthur refused to work with Doc Maynard. Even when the doctor made clear-headed sober-sided sense in his suggestion about which direction the streets should run.

The Turbulent Years

THE SMOOTHLY COMPETENT DOC MAYNARD understood something about the character of the American people that only recently has been clearly articulated: We are more interested in the idea of a thing than in the thing itself. This is why public relations is a growth industry.

Risk-takers who capitalize on their luck have a knack for PR.

In Doc Maynard's day, the people in the Pacific Northwest knew absolutely that the first town to get a steam sawmill would become the major metropolis.

Every town north of the Columbia River — and there were a dozen or more struggling to survive — needed a steam sawmill worse than it needed anything on earth. All those little towns had hopes of growing up to be the major metropolis. But only one of those towns had Doc Maynard.

Maynard understood that he had to get a steam sawmill for his town. He couldn't have cared less whether that mill cut boards straight enough for the San Francisco lumber trade. All he cared about was getting a steam sawmill here first so that people perceived Seattle as having an edge.

He heard about a fellow Ohioan named Henry Yesler who was

headed west with all the parts for a steam sawmill. By giving Yesler a choice chunk of land, Maynard persuaded him to put his mill together in Seattle.

Because he brought his sawmill parts to us in 1852, Yesler has been dubbed the economic father of our city. Never mind that he took five months to assemble those parts, a process that took a crew of normal competence a week. Never mind that he took more from the city than he ever gave.

At least he provided the steam sawmill that boosted Seattle further toward becoming the Queen City of the Pacific.

Another bit of perceived wisdom in Doc Maynard's day was that the first Puget Sound town to be listed as a railroad terminus in the government survey would rapidly become the major metropolis.

Maynard went into action again.

He sold an entire block of his claim to a fallen-away Quaker, who built a mock antebellum mansion, the fanciest structure on Puget Sound, and turned it over to Madam Damnable and her troops. A more-splendid-than-anything-else whorehouse in a struggling city is in the same category as the farmer's barn built on a grander scale than his home.

Madam Damnable was the name bestowed on Mary Ann Boyer by sailors from the far corners of the earth. Pretty soon the railroad survey crew knew her name, too.

In 1853, Doc Maynard's town was the terminus listed in the railroad report.

Maynard was racing other town fathers to look the best. He sold land on the condition that the new owner put up a building of certain dimensions. He didn't care what the back of the building looked like. The street fronts were what counted . . . sort of like a Metro-Goldwyn-Mayer movie set. It was a race against time.

Seattle looked bigger and fancier faster than its dowdy sister cities on Puget Sound.

It was the "fustest with the mostest."

When the booze went after Doc Maynard's liver (as it did the livers of a good many men who had served our city brilliantly), Seattle missed his generally kindly but firm guiding hand. You see, while Doc was our benevolent dictator until his death in 1873, most of the landowners sat on their hands while he did the things that made them rich . . . like engineering the Indian treaty which gave us just about all of the land in today's city limits.

And he had to negotiate around and through a territorial governor whose notion of how best to handle the Indians could be described in two words: Exterminate them.

The guv wasn't that drastic when he was sober.

But then he wasn't sober that often.

Bagley's Brass

As Seattle moved into the second decade (1860–1870), we seemed to have a healthy start on being the major metropolis of the Pacific Northwest.

During the 1860s we managed to engineer two more mainstays of our future.

A mild-mannered salubrious Methodist minister named Daniel H. Bagley arrived on the scene with a dream of starting a university.

He browbeat the parsimonious Arthur Denny into giving up prime property, and he snatched authority from a Legislature that never saw him coming.

In 1860 Seattle had about 200 inhabitants. The biggest financial plum the U.S. government had to offer a territory was a land grant of 20,000 acres, which could be sold to finance a university.

The minimum price for an acre of that land was set at $1.50. And somebody had to donate ten acres as a site for the university before the grant would go through.

Bagley persuaded Denny to be the land donor. Tightwad Arthur first tried to give Bagley the slide area on the hill just below today's Pike Place Market.

Bagley, however, had his eye on the best piece of view property on Denny's donation claim. On April 16, 1861, Denny signed a quit claim deed to eight and one-third acres, the site of today's Four Seasons-Olympic Hotel and other choice real estate. Two other settlers kicked in the land to bring Bagley's holdings up to the requisite ten acres.

Next, Bagley started selling off the 20,000-acre land grant. He didn't exactly have legislative permission. He did have buyers, though, willing to pay the $1.50 an acre. Most of his business came from timber companies.

By the time the legislature decided to put a stop to his activities, he had sold all the land and spent nearly all the $30,000 on buildings.

Nobody knew quite how it happened.

But there it was . . .

Like the Convention Center straddling Interstate 5 today.

Men have got to have something to do . . .

We all know that.

When irate members of a legislative investigating committee showed up in Seattle to put a stop to Bagley's university-building activities, they were met by a brass band and invited to participate in the dedication ceremonies.

There wasn't a man, woman or child in Seattle with enough education to qualify for entrance into a university. For years, we used Bagley's boondoggle as a high school.

The important thing was that we had stolen the University of Washington away from some of the would-be big-time cities like Port Townsend, Olympia and Vancouver.

Let's see . . .

The U of Dub . . .

How much does it bring in annually . . .

A billion, five hundred million . . .

Not counting eggheads.

Wow!

That's a university its football team can be proud of.

Seward's Bronze

The other big event of the 1860s for Seattle was her prominent role in the acquisition of her most important hinterland . . .

The state of Alaska.

This magoozle took more than a lousy thirty thousand.

We're talking this time about seven million.

What we did was strike while the iron was hot.

This one was pure luck.

We didn't know the iron was even there, let alone hot. But it was a memorial (a statement of facts addressed to a government, often accompanied by a petition or remonstrance) initiated in Seattle that got Secretary of State William Seward going on the purchase of the ice box . . .

And provided us with a nice bronze likeness of Secretary Seward to grace Volunteer Park.

Alaska was purchased by the United States not because of its strategic importance or great mineral resources (gold had not as yet been discovered there) but because some goddamn Russian fishermen would not let some Ballard fishermen use the toilet facilities at Sitka.

The Russians were downright dirty about even letting us catch fish around Sitka.

So in January of 1866, we got a memorial through the territorial legislature asking President Andrew Johnson either to get the Navy after those rude Russians or to buy Alaska.

Seward closed the deal on October 18, 1867, and Alaska has been a wholly owned subsidiary of Seattle ever since.

The turbulent decade had a few other things going for it, although you have to admit that the purchase of Alaska was not bad. We failed to get the Sandwich Islands (now known as Hawaii) annexed, but we would keep on trying for another thirty years and finally succeed.

We had to dis-incorporate our city to get rid of Henry Yesler as our mayor, which started the rumblings about initiative and recall and referendum and jail terms for public officials.

Most of what we did had its origins in religion . . .

"The Lord helps those who help themselves."

Lord, help us all.

Railroaded

*I*T IS NOT SURPRISING that after the halcyon days of the 1860s, when almost nothing went wrong except Henry Yesler, it was time for us to get our butt burned.

And get it burned we did.

It is terribly tempting to blame a small-town thinker for the debacle, but as my wife is endlessly pointing out, that's like getting mad at our airedale for not answering the telephone.

All of Seattle was in the habit of getting something for nothing. Doc Maynard had taken care of us. He got us listed as the terminus of the transcontinental railroad in territorial Governor Isaac I. Stevens' thirteen-volume report on the Northern Pacific route. Edwin Ferry Johnson, railroader extraordinaire, had flatly stated that Seattle would become the Queen City of the Pacific and no power on earth could stop it.

When Johnson was hired as the chief engineer of the Northern Pacific, he named Seattle as the terminus of the transcontinental railroad, which was just reiterating what everyone had taken for granted for the past twenty years.

Arthur Denny was put in charge of the reception committee for the Northern Pacific Railroad. That's what the city's guiding lights figured they needed . . . a reception committee. The railroad was going through Snoqualmie Pass, like people had been saying ever since the subject came up in the early 1850s. All we had to do was get out the red, white and blue bunting and strike up the band.

Right?

Wrong!

Drunk or sober, Doc Maynard would have told them that in the city-building business you kill flies with sledgehammers. Unfortunately, Doc Maynard was dead.

Three months after Maynard died, Arthur Denny got a telegram from two Northern Pacific Railroad commissioners:

"We have located the terminus on Commencement Bay."

Wait a minute . . .

Isn't Commencement Bay in Tacoma?

The bad news came on July 14, 1873.

Nobody should have been surprised.

The Northern Pacific Railroad people had started a little enterprise called the Tacoma Land Company. So the tail wagged the dog.

The Tacoma Land Company owned Tacoma, lock, stock and whatever that third thing is.

Since the same people who owned Tacoma were empowered to decide where to put the terminus of the Northern Pacific Railroad, what site do you suppose they chose?

They followed the same site selection criteria all across the country. The land company owned a chunk of property two miles north of Yakima, so that's where the station was to be.

But wait another minute.

Ellensburg's Beef

Ellensburg had something to prove here, namely that the Northern Pacific people would go out of their way to make a buck.

Ellensburg was owned and operated by Dexter Horton. Ellensburg was the chief source of the Puget Sound supply of steaks.

"If you don't come to us," Horton quietly told the construction side of the company, "we'll drive our steers over Snoqualmie Pass on the hoof to Puget Sound and slaughter them there."

I would be willing to bet that Dexter was burnishing his fingernails on his coat lapel while he casually drew attention to the empire builders' dilemma.

And the dilemma was something.

Here was the biggest shipper of the most desirable commodity on Puget Sound—sizzler steaks for he-men.

He wanted the railroad on land in which the Northern Pacific had no financial stake.

What would you do if you were a board member of both the railroad-building and the land-grabbing companies?

Easy answer?

Of course!

They routed the track a couple of miles out of the way to take care of Dexter Horton's beef . . . and then routed it back to Stampede Pass so the trains would emerge in Tacoma, which, of course, the Northern Pacific land company was planning to make into the major city on Puget Sound.

Just lovely?

I'll say!

Everybody was happy.

Or were they?

What about Arthur Denny, the guy in charge of bringing the railroad to Seattle?

Not so you could notice.

Before Northern Pacific announced its terminus, Seattle had a population of 1,500 and was the largest town on Puget Sound. Tacoma had about 100 lost souls.

After the announcement, Seattle's population drained south, just as sure as if somebody had pulled the plug. It dropped overnight to 500, while Tacoma's people count rose to . . .

Guess what?

Fifteen hundred.

One of Seattle's leading citizens, in fact he was our mayor for two terms, left for Tacoma when he got an offer to build that budding metropolis' first hotel.

Arthur Denny was beside himself. He had been fooled.

He hadn't a clue about the Northern Pacific's betrayal of Seattle.

His partner in the bank of Seattle was Dexter Horton.

The fellow who had gotten the Northern Pacific's attention in Ellensburg.

Dexter Horton had not bothered to tell Arthur Denny about his own negotiations with the railroad.

His own business partner had kept Arthur in the dark.

May Day, May Day

Denny decided he would build his own railroad through Snoqualmie Pass to Walla Walla, where he would hook up with the Union Pacific.

He called for volunteer labor. The men of the town would set aside one day a week for the building of the railroad. They would be paid in railroad stock. They would show the world the kind of spirit Seattle had.

And they did.

That's where we get the myth of the famous May Day picnic. May 1, 1874, all businesses and schools closed, and everyone turned out to help Arthur Denny build his railroad.

The heck to pieces with the Northern Pacific and Tacoma.

Ooh, boy!

Henry Yesler, who was whittling while the others entertained themselves with picks and shovels, shouted out: "Quit your fooling and get to work."

And work they did . . .

For one afternoon.

After that, the Seattle spirit was willing, but the flesh was weak.

The volunteers drifted back to their jobs.

Denny, as president of the board of the Seattle and Walla Walla Railroad, had gotten as far as buying a small locomotive named the Arthur A. Denny.

But there was somebody else in town, a guy who gets scant attention in most of our history books. His name was James H. Colman . . . a thrifty man of few words and lots of ability. He had worked for some San Francisco financiers who regarded his judgment and capacity for getting things done with deep respect.

Those same financiers were also aware that Seattle businessmen had got to squabbling among themselves over who would control the coal mines on the other side of Lake Washington . . .

And lost them to San Francisco interests.

Arthur Denny needed money to finance his railroad.

James Colman needed a project to challenge his superintending skills.

The San Francisco financiers needed a less expensive way to move coal from the King County mines fifteen or twenty miles to the Seattle harbor.

Colman's idea was simplicity itself.

Forget Walla Walla and make tracks for the mines.

But what about the name? Seattle and Walla Walla?

What's in a name?

"Mr. Denny, sir, if you like I would be happy to take all the risks by relieving you of responsibility for the Seattle and Walla Walla Railroad."

"You would!" Then more carefully, with a touch of indifference: "You would?"

"Of course, I have only two or three peanuts to spend."

Denny wavered.

How about four big goobers?

"Sold." Followed by a sigh of relief.

"Including the locomotive."

"Including the locomotive . . . " Sigh (nostalgia, this time).

"Be happy to leave your name on it."

Ironically, it was May Day, 1876, when Colman's paid laborers went to work on building a railroad. The following March, Colman was at the throttle when the train pulled into Renton.

Later he extended the line seven miles north to Newcastle, where the richest mine operated.

That King County coal made Colman a multimillionaire and gave Arthur Denny somebody besides Doc Maynard to hate.

Joshua Green & the Mosquito Fleet

Mosquitoes Kill Tacoma

C OLMAN'S ROAD was barely a harassment to the beleaguered Northern Pacific. It was the lunatics operating little ships called the Mosquito Fleet who really punctured plans to make Tacoma the major city on Puget Sound.

The Mosquito Fleet was composed of hundreds of little ships—most of them really quite small indeed, less than one hundred feet long—which swarmed wherever the money was on Puget Sound or the waters tributary to it.

The Mosquito Fleet was the greatest conglomeration of ships and boats in the world, ranging from magnificent liners hauling hundreds of passengers to amazing box-like contraptions that carried things and moved on water. They were sawed in two and lengthened . . . or sawed off and shortened. They were sleek and cantankerous, stubby and profitable. They allegedly could run on heavy dew. They blew up, sank, ran into piers, other boats and the shore. They made men rich and sent them to the poorhouse.

Anyone who had a bright idea about what constituted a boat, and also had some lumber, nuts, bolts and ingenuity (or the wherewithal to hire someone with lumber, nuts, bolts and ingenuity) could put one of them together and become a captain in the early days. These captains who didn't know the first thing about navigating on water caused a lot of collisions and damaged piers, so ultimately the federal government made up a test that became a prerequisite to the rank. A lot of captains had to give up their ships. Usually, they did not give up their title, which was something most of them retained for the rest of their days. Anybody who was anybody was a captain on Puget Sound. It was like being a colonel in the South.

It was a Southerner, in fact, who made the Mosquito Fleet Seattle's biggest booster of the late nineteenth century.

In 1886, when the sixteen-year-old Joshua Green arrived in Seattle from Mississippi, our city and Tacoma were nearly even in population at about 8,000 people each.

Two years after his arrival in the Northwest, Green became purser on the Henry Bailey, a 108-foot-long boat that was based in Tacoma and carried supplies to loggers as far up the Skagit River as it could travel. The Henry Bailey was owned by the Pacific Navigation Company, which had won the mail contract between Seattle and Tacoma. Pacific Navigation was based in Tacoma and was one of the strongest and biggest outfits in the Mosquito Fleet.

Even though he started his shipping career in Tacoma, Green held no allegiance to that city.

From Rat City to Brat City

But wait a minute. Maybe it would be polite here to introduce someone who was loyal to Tacoma, someone to say a word on her behalf.

From time to time, we hear a little whining about how we treat Tacoma on our Underground Tour. So I guess it's only fair that we bring on Ezra Meeker, who, on behalf of Tacoma, gave Seattle the nickname during the 1880s that was right on target.

Meeker, the great publicist for the Oregon Trail, first noted that "you could smell Seattle five miles before you could see it." Then he dropped the other shoe, the one that really fit. He tagged Seattle "Brat City."

Other people had been referring to us as "Rat City" because of the oversupply of rats in the garbage dumps that comprised seventy-five percent of what today is Pioneer Square.

After Doc Maynard died, no one was really running the show. Henry Yesler, who served a couple of terms as mayor, was by all odds the biggest burglar of the bunch. He couldn't make his mill profitable, but he figured out how to bleed the city dry. And he did have clout with city hall.

For instance, on January 18, 1882, three men were lynched in his front yard. He had the feeling that national headlines reading "THREE LYNCHED IN SEATTLE BUSINESS DISTRICT" would give the city a bad name. So he had the health department report changed to list the cause of death as "irate citizens."

In 1882, the health commissioner complained that twice a day when the tide came in the major trunk sewers reversed their flow and flush toilets became fountains. He recommended that the streets be raised so gravity could keep the sewage down. He also pointed out that Seattle had the highest death rate in the nation.

Henry ignored most of the commissioner's report, but he was moved to act on the death rate statistic. In disregard of the census, he raised the population figure, thereby lowering the death rate to a more respectable number.

On June 6, 1889, many of the city's health problems were solved when the entire central business district burned to the ground. A million rats were killed. When new streets were built, they were raised, giving the sewage a one-way passage to the sea.

The fire was our first great urban renewal project.

Sitting on His Fannie

While the city was burning, Joshua Green was not fiddling around. He was thinking about buying his own boat, a funny little thing called the Fannie Lake. She looked like a scow with a big box, topped by a smaller box, topped by a deluxe model outhouse. She had been built in Seattle in 1874. She also had been a little money-maker in the White River trade. Toward the end of 1889, Green had talked her owner into selling her for $5,000.

Times were tough in those days, and Green couldn't put together five thousand cents, let alone five thousand dollars. So he had some little chats with his fellow crew members on the Henry Bailey, with Sam Denny, the captain; Peter Falk, the first mate; and Frank Zikmund, the engineer. The four men went to see Jacob Furth at Puget Sound National Bank. They wondered if they could borrow $1,250 apiece in order to buy this magnificent money-making specimen of the Mosquito Fleet. They comprised the crew necessary to operate the vessel at a profit, and they were willing to work their fool heads off doing it.

Furth looked each of the young men in the eye and then said: "Yes, I'll loan you the money, and I think you'll pay it back, too."

The Fannie Lake paid for herself two or three times over in the first year. Green and company began to buy up other little boats. They worked around the clock. The boats went anywhere and everywhere to pick up or deliver a few tons of cargo — hay and grain, peevees, saws and axes, processed foods, rubber boots, nails, beer, rope, donkey engines, plows, shovels, fish nets, knitting needles, thread, yarn, pots and pans, beef, coal, lumber, poultry, vegetables.

Joshua Green traces the making of his personal fortune to the day when he got a bright idea that gave him as much of a leg up on the competition as Henry Yesler's steam sawmill gave Seattle.

When Green first went to work on the Mosquito Fleet, it was the custom of all the little boats to go up the rivers and sloughs north of Seattle at high tide. The farmers all had landings where the boats would tie up. When the tide went out, the boats lay in the mud at the landing for eighteen hours, until the next high tide. They would be loaded in the meantime.

Green worked out a new system where he could get in and load and get out on the same tide. When I interviewed him in 1966, a bit before his ninety-seventh birthday, he explained his time-saving method this way:

> In the middle of the summer, you know, most of the high tides are during the night. Well, those farmers worked hard all day . . . and they liked to get a good night's sleep. We'd come along about two o'clock in the morning and wake them up to help us load so we could make the tide. They didn't like that very well. They called me 'public nuisance number one.' But we kidded them along and we'd all work hard together and get the ship loaded. It took about three hours for the whole operation.

Green's eighteen-hour jump on those other boats lolling around in the mud gave him the extra profits that allowed him to lower his bids on the mail contracts. A mail contract was worth from twenty to twenty-five percent of the total cost of a passenger run. The guy who got the mail contract was in an invulnerable position when it came to a rate war. Green ended up with most of the mail contracts on most of the big, profitable routes.

He worked a little harder. He thought a little shrewder. And he made a fortune. In the process, he gave Seattle the edge on the other towns in Puget Sound. With Joshua Green and the Mosquito Fleet, we have another case where the risk-taker, the location and the timing all came together.

When he was new in the shipping trade, young Mr. Green didn't spend his spare time lying in his bunk on the Henry Bailey snoozing. He was a man who kept his eyes open, his ears alert and his brain awake. Possibly without realizing the important role he was playing, he dropped one of the last pieces into the jigsaw puzzle that was making economic history on Puget Sound.

The first few ships of the Mosquito Fleet operated out of Olympia, at the head of the sound and the most important city because it was near the Chehalis Valley and tromping up from the Columbia River was fairly easy. Roads came in early. Olympia was the capital and that sort of thing. The mail contract, which was so important, went from Olympia to Port Townsend, with a stop in Seattle.

Tacoma didn't even exist.

Then the Northern Pacific came into Tacoma and provided the fastest route to Portland, which was by far and away the biggest city in the Pacific Northwest.

While Green was purser on the Henry Bailey, he noted a couple of interesting things. More than fifty percent of the whole population of the state lived directly west and north of Seattle right on Puget Sound. The Henry Bailey was based in Tacoma, but most of its cargoes were destined to go north of Seattle.

The Henry Bailey made no stops between Seattle and Tacoma. It took three hours to make the trip between the two cities. These were three wasted hours. By basing his boats in Seattle, Green could make four trips a week. In Tacoma, he was limited to three trips.

The original owner of the Pacific Navigation Company died. The operation of the company devolved on a Tacoma law firm, the members of which probably were not spending twenty-four hours a day figuring out how to make a better deal, more money, the way Joshua

Green was. Eventually, Green took over Pacific Navigation. Most of the Mosquito Fleet was then based in Seattle.

"It wasn't that we loved Tacoma less, but that we loved the dividends more," was the way Green viewed the decision to base his boats in Seattle.

Going Furth Class

Joshua Green knew where to turn when he had courage but no capital. He got in line with all the others for a fifteen-minute interview with banker Jacob Furth.

Furth's risk-taking judgment was the best to come to Seattle in its first half century.

The way he applied that judgment made him the city's leading citizen for thirty years.

He may even have been the most important citizen Seattle ever had.

He also may be the most unrecognized number one citizen Seattle ever had.

All Jacob Furth did was take a squalid little village named Seattle and turn it into a world class city. He made good on Doc Maynard's dream.

He was an unflappable Bohemian gentleman known for his sartorial splendor and his uncanny accuracy in sizing people up. He had a brisk moustache and a pointed beard. His body, broad of shoulder, exuded health. His calm eyes stripped men's minds of thoughts that some of them didn't even know they had.

Jacob Furth arrived in Seattle in 1882. He was forty-two years old.

He had come to this country when he was eighteen. The flame was in him. And the challenge was in America. So he left his family in

Bohemia and traveled to San Francisco with letters of introduction to the Schwabacher Brothers, merchants. They eyed the earnest little foreigner with "show me" skepticism and sent him to work in a drygoods store in Nevada City, California.

He was a clerk, working mornings and evenings. During the day, he went to school to learn English. When the Schwabachers checked up on him after his first six months, he was speaking better English than they were.

He was making forty dollars a month in Nevada City. He managed to save half of that. He put some of his money into a quicksilver mine. He admitted to "living frugally."

The Schwabachers began to view the young Bohemian with respect. The watched carefully as he plugged away at his drygoods job for five long years. When the store burned down, he went to work in a general store in Shingle Springs and stayed there for five years.

Then he thought he might like to strike out on his own. The Schwabachers offered him financing.

No thank you very much, he told them. He had saved enough on his own.

He bought into a general merchandise business that operated a branch in Colusa, California. After eight years, the newest partner was ready to buy out everyone else. The historical society in Colusa still has a picture of Jacob Furth's store and lists him as one of the town's most important pioneers.

Colusa's loss

But the Colusa climate didn't agree with him, and ill health forced him to quit the general merchandise business and look for another line of work.

He had heard about good business opportunities in a place called Puget Sound. The by now extremely friendly Schwabacher Brothers told him more. They were supplying the ships of the Mosquito Fleet.

The little town of Seattle was holding its own against the seemingly powerful Northern Pacific Railroad, which had been trying for ten years to put it out of business.

"We are contemplating opening a bank in Seattle," the Schwabacher Brothers said to Furth. "As long as you're planning to go into business there anyway, how would you like to throw in your lot with us? Bailey

Gatzert, our man in Seattle will, of course, be president. But we need somebody to be everybody else."

"Mutter und Vater," the ecstatic Furth wrote to the folks back in Austria, "I finally have been accepted by the Schwabacher Brothers!"

It had taken only twenty-five years.

In August of 1883, Furth opened Puget Sound National Bank, with $50,000 capital.

He put his bank in the wilds of First Avenue South and Yesler Way. This was the northern end of the central business district and the up-and-coming area of the city at the time.

Here one found dry land, which was an inducement to commerce. Doc Maynard had started the central business district thirty years earlier with his store, the Seattle Exchange, two blocks south at Main Street.

The first civic duty Furth performed was reassembling our water system, which had just gone belly up. This led to the water system that today supplies eighty percent of everyone in King County.

Furth had been here only a couple of months. For a man who claimed to have moved to Seattle to repair his health, Furth moved with amazing grace into a pattern that would become his hallmark . . . repairing broken business ventures.

Pipe Dreams

From the founding of the city, there had been a series of unsuccessful attempts to consolidate the different water systems. In 1881, the Spring Hill Water System was the latest of those efforts. That system went full speed ahead . . . broke.

Brand new to town, Jacob Furth picked up the pieces at Seattle's first yard sale. He persuaded Bailey Gatzert, his banking colleague and head of the biggest wholesale and retail mercantile firm north of San Francisco, and John Leary, founder of the Post-Intelligencer and all-around capitalist, to throw in with him and take over the Spring Hill system. Within a year, they announced plans to double the size of the system and to start pumping water from Lake Washington where the Mount Baker bathing beach is today. They might have gone on indefinitely, expanding the system as Seattle's population burgeoned, but for an unfortunate incident in 1889.

An overturned pot of glue set off a fire that appeared at first to be controllable. A fire engine hooked up to the hydrant at First and Columbia and laid two lines of hose. The crowd started to cheer as the fireman turned two mighty streams of water toward the fire. The cheers turned to gasps when the water turned from a gush to a weak spurting that would not reach the top of the building.

The entire central business district burned and any hope for the continued existence of a privately owned water system in Seattle turned to ashes.

To this day no one knows why that hydrant failed. It was not for lack of water in the reservoirs or lack of pumping power. Probably somebody way down below Gatzert, Leary and Furth in the water system made the kind of mistake they haven't even yet found an eraser for.

The people saw only the disastrous failure of the water system. They wanted the blood of Spring Hill.

Furth was not one to fight overwhelming popular sentiment. When he saw the writing on the wall, he added his signature to it.

He bucked the business establishment and worked behind the scenes with the city council in support of city engineer R. H. Thomson, who was fighting for a publicly owned, gravity-flow water system from the Cedar River...

Furth forgot about his own interests and sided with Thomson. Even though Thomson, with his unbridled ambition to level every hill in Seattle so that we looked like Kansas City instead of falling into the trap of being as beautiful as San Francisco, had already reached deeper into the pockets of the city's business leaders than capitalist decency allowed.

Furth and J. J. McGilvra, the dean of the Seattle Bar Association, were the only two establishment figures who defected to the side of the public in the water supply battle.

When one city council member was the last holdout against public ownership of the system, Furth was approached about persuading him otherwise. Furth stared at the petitioner with those calm, clear, kindly eyes and finally said: "Mr. Thomson has cost us a great deal of money. But this time he's right. I'll see what I can do in the matter."

The recalcitrant councilman changed his mind about Thomson's plan. In 1895 voters approved a bond issue financing the Cedar River water supply system.

A Neglected Giant

When Jacob Furth died on June 2, 1914, he commanded the longest, most praise-filled obituary ever printed in the Seattle press, before or since.

For all practical purposes, he ran the show here from 1883 until he died. Yet there are no streets, statues, parks or public buildings to honor him. He made fewer headlines than most, which means that he gets scant mention in our history books.

He was not one to toot his own horn. He came from a part of the world where men refrained from telling their right hands what their left hands were doing.

When Welford Beaton tried writing Furth's biography, he ended up with a book called The City That Made Itself and dedicated it to Furth. He found when he finished studying Furth, he knew less about him than when he started.

Furth began the proceedings with Beaton by saying:

> *What we want is a story about the fights the city had to make itself; the people who will read it are not concerned with the birthplace of any of the men who engaged in the fights or how old they are now or were at the time of their death. And also let us have one volume that will not be full of the portraits of those who were willing to buy their way into it and a eulogy of those who are prepared to purchase it.*

Furth's self-effacing style has resulted in his being neglected in the written history of our city.

But as the nineteenth century and Seattle's first fifty years came to a close, no one was more important to the direction the city would take.

Jacob Furth, in partnership with Seattle's first and most successful business woman and with a brash empire builder from Minnesota, fulfilled all of Doc Maynard's vision for the town on Puget Sound.

Jacob Furth at his desk

Oh, Henry!

*I*N 1885, when Jacob Furth was elected to the city council for the first and only time he chose to run for public office, the voters saw fit to elect Henry Yesler as our mayor . . .

For the second time!

Which just goes to show you that when you think you have the voters of Seattle figured out, you'd better start figuring again.

Twenty years earlier, we had elected Henry as our mayor and then been forced to dis-incorporate in order to get rid of him. After we re-incorporated, Henry proved in court that we had done it the wrong way. And he was the only one who didn't have to pay his assessment for the first regrading of First Avenue. This pushed the city to the verge of bankruptcy.

So we elected him mayor again.

It's pretty hard to get into the voters' minds, but the only reason I can offer for his election was his colorful language. You see, we had just held the last lynching party in the city . . . three men in some maple trees in Henry's front yard. As you will recall, Henry got the cause of death listed as irate citizens.

Of the event, which he had witnessed whilst whittling, Henry was quoted as saying, "That was the first fruit them trees ever bore, but it was the finest."

Quotes like that, plus the all-day sucker formed in his image (one of the most unusual campaign buttons in history) made him irresistible to voters.

Henry Yesler was one of Jacob Furth's civic projects.

Even though Henry had substantial real estate assets, he had a serious cash flow problem. He had a weakness for con men blowing into town with get-rich-quick schemes. He got into the habit of co-signing notes with these characters. When they had sense enough to leave town before being run out, they left Henry to pay their bills. All his property was mortgaged to the limit.

Henry's nephew J. D. Lowman, who stood to inherit his uncle's estate, if anything was left, went to Jacob Furth to see what could be done to keep Henry from squandering any more of his money. Furth, whom everyone trusted, got Henry to sign over all his property. Furth became Henry's business manager.

This was in 1887.

Lest you be worried that Henry, who was 70 years old at the time, was reduced to going hat in hand to the bank and begging for his allowance, let me reassure you.

He had an arrangement with a man named Gamma Poncin. When Henry needed money, Poncin would oblige him. Poncin was so sensitive of Henry's pride that he agreed not to nag him about repayment of these loans. He would just seek repayment, with interest, from the Yesler estate. That way, when the indelicate matter of debt came up, Henry would be far removed from material concerns.

So you see, Henry did not have to cut back on the style of living to which he had become accustomed. In fact, he managed to become accustomed to an even more lavish style.

A Scandal Monger's Delight

In 1887, when his wife died, he decided he needed the biggest mansion in town. He spent $50,000 on a delightful monstrosity of wood, which he kept populated by a strange collection of characters. His menage, in fact, kept the town's scandal mongers busy.

Just how busy they were is indicated in a letter written to Henry in 1890. This letter was part of a collection of Yesler letters that the

Washington State Historical Society purchased in 1985 from a rare book dealer in New York State.

The letter is reprinted here in its entirety and in all of its solicitude, with original spelling intact. It is dated November 10, 1890, and addressed to "My old pioneer friend:"

> *I have been thinking for a long time that I would like to write you a letter as I have much to say that is of importance to you. I thought that a few friendly words would not offend you if they were given in a spirit of kindness, and our heads are to white now with age to get angry over a little piece of advise one may give the other. I felt a great deal of sorow for you when your dear companion was taken away from you and you were left alone in your old age, but I have felt a greater grief to hear the tonges of scandal pointed towards you in the way they have been for the past two years and that you may now the magnitude of it I thought I would write you this letter to warn you that unless some quick measures be taken by yourself you will lose the respect of the community of Seattle. The story that is going round is that you sleep with that girl you have at your house and that she has been with child by you several times and you have had it doctered away, that you took her east to have an opperation performed on her, that you have two girls at your house that you sleep with, and that you want to mary one of them, and that you make her fine presents and give her money for rong purposes. Now my old friend all this I don't believe about you. But so the story gose, and I am not able to stop it. I think you have command of to much common sense and honor to do all this, and I believe you to have to much selfrespet to want to mary a young girl against her will, as the story goes, or to want to ruin her caracter. All this talk is rong and should be avoided by every means at your command. There is no reason in the world why you should not mary. You are not to old. You should have a companion to comfort you in your old age. I no how it is, but you should find some women of maturer years, suited to your age, who can comfort you in sickness and bee a true companion in times of helth. This a yong girl cant do it is not naturel for a yung girl to love an old man for a husband. She is only an orniment in a house while you need sombody more substanshul, and my advise to you*

is, under the present circumstances, would bee to mary some good woman that is kapable to preside over your house, and then you can adopt this girl as your dauter and give her a home with you and let her bee a orniment in your home. Then the vile tonges of scandal will sease to wag about you. And you continue to have the respect of the people as I believe you still deserve. Now my old time friend, I hope you will take all I have writen you in kindnes for I mean no rong in writing you. I will not make myself known to you then you will not no with whom to be angry.

The letter is signed "Yours truley." Henry kept it until he died in 1892. He did not, however, take the "advise" of his anonymous friend.

The year he got the letter, he married the "orniment." She was fifty-five years younger than the eighty-year-old Henry.

Jacob Furth had much to sort out in handling the Henry Yesler estate. An office door labeled "Henry Yesler Estate" still was in the Pioneer Building a decade or so ago when that magnificent edifice was so lovingly and thoughtfully restored by architect Ralph Anderson.

The first repayment on Gamma Poncin's loans was a check for $37,540.06. Later on when the creditors of the estate had to form a corporation to prevent everything from going to the lawyers, Poncin was the biggest stockholder and was named president of the Henry Yesler Estate, Inc.

Sinning in the Rain

J ACOB FURTH was Seattle's most creative banker. His silent
partner in the banking business was Seattle's most successful
business woman. Between them, they gambled on the young
entrepreneurs who had the courage but not the capital to turn Seattle
into the Queen City of the Pacific.

Mr. Furth's silent partner was born Dorothea Georgine Emile
Ohben in Germany. She was known to her adopted town as Lou
Graham.

She arrived in Seattle in the late 1880s with a small amount of capital,
a burning ambition to become rich and the necessary training in her
field to do it.

Separating the facts from the legend surrounding this enterprising
woman takes us from the standard history books, which do not acknowledge her existence. We have to listen to our aural historians and
read the old newspapers and the actual court records and even make a
visit to the Department of Public Health in San Francisco.

All we know with absolute certainty is that Lou Graham was born
on February 9, 1857, and that she died in San Francisco on March 11,
1903.

And as in the ongoing saga of Henry Yesler, where he runs the gamut from saint to sinner depending on which pages of which book undertake a description of him, so it is with Lou Graham.

I wrote a chapter on Henry twenty years ago that would have been more to the point had I inserted the word "Dumb" between "The" and "Bastard."

My twenty-year-old chapter on Lou Graham, "The Hostess With the Mostest," was aptly titled, only at the time I was unaware of just how much she contributed to the development of our city.

Sometime in late 1887 or early 1888—it doesn't much matter which—Seattle's first first-class madam paid a call on the city's most creative banker.

He was forty-eight years old, and she was thirty-one.

He was sitting in his office on the main floor of a bank with a door that was open to all, usually from seven in the morning until that same hour in the evening. Furth, a workaholic, tried to see forty or fifty people a day, six days a week.

At the time Furth had been happily married for twenty-three years to a woman who worshipped him. Out of that union were three daughters, who knelt at the same altar as their mother.

Furth was never too busy to listen patiently to their domestic problems. Being a Bohemian gentleman, he loved and cared for his family. But, as was the custom in Bohemia, gentlemen relaxed with their mistresses, or played cards.

Mr. Furth preferred cards.

He knew that other men preferred mistresses.

Dressed for Success

For her meeting with the influential Mr. Furth, Lou Graham was wearing a black dress and a large hat with a bird wing along the crown, the latest fashion. Her jewelry, Furth noticed, was not paste. The diamonds had been selected by a person of exquisite taste.

The woman stood about five feet, two inches . . . and at chest height, she was about three feet thick. She had jet black hair and blue eyes, a prominent nose and a wide mouth.

She had swept regally into his office and wasted no small talk as he offered her a chair. Since he usually allowed only fifteen minutes for an interview, she would like to get down to business, she informed him crisply.

While Seattle had the usual complement of bawdyhouses, the town had not a single parlor house, she explained to the attentive banker. She spoke to him in his native tongue. Her accent indicated quality upbringing.

She told him she had paid $3,000 for a corner lot at Third Avenue South and South Washington Street and was prepared to furnish Seattle with the kind of first-class establishment that was proliferating in San Francisco.

She would provide a place where visiting dignitaries could find a little bit of quiet music and relaxation from their arduous travels in the company of lovely, intelligent, understanding women.

She proposed a multi-storied building. A fine parlor would be located on the first floor for those who sought no more than a quiet drink and pleasant companionship from the women who could discuss opera, or politics, or economics, or world conditions. For those who felt the need of deeper therapy, commodious quarters would be provided in the upper floors.

She would charge $2 across the board for a man wanting complete anonymity on the upper floor, and $5 for those who wished to spend the night — a sum that compared favorably with the best hotels in town. If for any reason a man had to seek the services of a physician after a visit to her establishment, she would pay the fee. The money and other valuables that the men carried would be as safe as if they were in Jacob Furth's bank.

What she needed from Mr. Furth involved a combination of banking, real estate and politics.

He was the quintessential representative of all three. He was the number-one banker. He knew real estate trends. And he was a member of the city council.

A Beautiful Friendship Begins

This first meeting between Lou Graham and Jacob Furth was the beginning of a beautiful friendship.

They both prospered.

They provided a vital combination of cash and compassion to the Seattle business community during the pivotal final decade of the nineteenth century.

When Jacob Furth felt that a young man was worthwhile but did not warrant risking banking principals, he sent the applicant with a note to Lou Graham. Lou would lend up to $500 at Furth's request.

Many a fortune belonging to our first families today grew out of a note sent by Furth to Lou saying that while he couldn't, under the scrutiny of a board of directors, make the loan, it was his judgment the man was good for it.

Lou's interest rates were outrageous, but when her judgment confirmed Furth's, the guy got the money.

Fire and Damnation

LOU GRAHAM was barely in business when the great urban renewal project sent Seattle into a frenzy. The fire of June 6, 1889, destroyed her parlor house at Third and Washington, along with the rest of the central business district.

Lou rebuilt right away. She plunked down cash for a three-story building that was about eight times more pretentious than her original establishment. She adhered to the new code stipulating that only brick and stone buildings could be constructed in the burned area.

Lou also started the property acquisitions that would leave a respectable estate when she died.

Some idea of the kind of wealth she had acquired during the eighteen months she had been in business before the fire wiped her out shows on the records. When she bought additional land after the fire, she paid $25,000 for it.

Those in Seattle who lacked Lou's resources had to find some way to restore what had been a promising start to a city.

Our history books refer to the mass meeting that was held on June 7, 1889, during which there was a unanimous vote to raise and widen the streets and build in Pioneer Square the finest city center in the United States.

Well, at least west of Chicago.

The question of how to pay for this magnificent city center was not discussed at the mass meeting of the city council. At a subsequent meeting of the city council, when the question of the cost for this wonderful project came up, the enthusiasm level dropped considerably.

What Seattle needed, which it had never needed before, was lots of money.

Thirty miles away sat Tacoma, where the Northern Pacific railroaders were gloating. They had promised to see the day when grass grew in Seattle's streets. After the fire, that day seemed imminent.

So Seattle's town fathers, including the business community, did what they always had done when they were in trouble.

They went to see Mr. Furth.

A Stream of Schemes

Every possible scheme for rebuilding the city streamed past Mr. Furth's appraising eyes. The line of men and their plans formed at seven o'clock in the morning and lasted until seven o'clock in the evening. They all wanted money.

The burden born by Jacob Furth would have killed a lesser man.

You see, he had to say no to ninety percent of the applicants.

Those he said yes to built a much grander city than the one that had been destroyed. The net result is what you see today in the Pioneer Square historic district.

The worth of the property that had burned was about $15 million. The reconstruction bill came to $150 million.

Relief funds of $120,000 poured in when the world learned of the fire.

That was not even enough to pay Henry Yesler for a piece of his property that the city wanted. Before the fire, First Avenue came south to Yesler Way where it was stopped by buildings. First Avenue South came north to Yesler Way where it, too, was stopped by buildings. What was needed was called "cutting the Yesler corner." This meant bending First Avenue toward the water and creating public property known today as the triangle on which the pergola, totem pole and Chief Seattle fountain stand.

Henry was happy to sell a piece of his land that would bring First Avenue together and give him some spending money. He got $156,000 for the 13,000 square feet the city needed. That figures out to be $12 a square foot.

Other property owners who had land condemned for public use got an average of 66 cents per square foot.

The bulk of the money to rebuild the city came from some hard-nosed San Francisco bankers who trusted Jacob Furth to see that they would not get burned in the deal.

Parlor Games

As the city got back on its feet, the center of government seemed to move into the first-floor parlor at Lou Graham's house.

It was Lou's policy that private booths and whatever libation suited the occasion always were available at no cost to representatives of Seattle's city government any time of the day or night.

More city business was transacted at Lou's than at city hall.

This was only appropriate because more city revenue came from Lou and her ilk than from any other source. In fact, for a time the city ran on fines from prostitutes and gamblers. Prostitutes were required to pay $10 a month. Gamblers paid $50 per month per gaming table. These funds operated the city . . . and had they not been there to pay there might not have been any city later on.

They contributed eighty-seven percent of the general fund until a new charter forced businessmen in less colorful occupations to pay their fair share.

Lou is another example of the risk-taker who appreciates the value of public relations.

Her principal method of advertising took the form of carriage rides up and down the main streets on a Sunday afternoon. Dressed in their best finery, the young ladies of her establishment were regularly put on display. And no man of distinction in Seattle had any difficulty in pointing out when a new girl had been added to the entourage.

Joshua Green told me that fathers took their sons to Lou Graham's as a college graduation present.

"It was considered an integral part of a young man's education," Green said.

And then, with arm and forefinger pointed heavenward, the old gentleman added: "But it stopped at the altar. You understand? IT STOPPED AT THE ALTAR."

The young men who continued their education at Lou Graham's did so without telling their mothers. Still, the women of the city knew what was going on. Most of them did not approve.

In 1890, they organized the Christian Committee to ferret out and save fallen women. Members of the Christian Committee got off their pedestals long enough to tromp the streets, urging salvation on their debased sisters.

The year the Christian Committee formed was also the year that a luckless fellow by the name of Harry White was asked to be mayor and to clean up the prostitution and gambling in the city. He went into action when the Christian Committee's efforts appeared to be having little effect.

On Valentine's Day, 1891, a rookie cop made sure that White's political career would be brief. He arrested Lou Graham.

Her two attorneys were among the most prominent men in town. J. T. Ronald would be the next elected mayor and a King County Superior Court judge for the last fifty years of his life. He had just completed a term as prosecuting attorney for the county.

Samuel Piles had been an assistant prosecuting attorney and would go on to be a U.S. senator

Shaking the Foundations

The day of Lou's trial, the streets were lined with onlookers. Lou arrived in her carriage. She was dressed to the teeth.

The courtroom was so packed with people that the building began to tremble. The judge ordered the crowd out, advising people to move slowly, so as not to shake the foundations.

The jury took three minutes to reach a verdict . . . not proven.

This disgusted the Seattle Press-Times, which railed:

> *Once more an intelligent police court jury has rendered the famous Scotch verdict of not proven and 'Madame' Lou Graham, the proprietress of the most notorious house of ill repute, the most gorgeous and sumptuously furnished palace of sin in the city, is released from custody. It is a palatial three-story brick building erected, at a large cost, from the wages of sin.*

Lou went back to collecting the wages of sin.
Harry White resigned his office, on the grounds of ill health.

Lou Graham in her carriage

Portrait of a Lady

WHEN LOU GRAHAM DIED UNEXPECTEDLY on a trip to San Francisco in 1903, Jacob Furth saw to it that the men who had diamonds, watches and money in her safe were able to retrieve their treasures with no embarrassing questions.

One of Furth's employees, R.V. Ankeny, became administrator of Lou's estate.

She left no will, and no one knew of any heirs or next of kin. Eventually, three people from Hamburg claimed to be two sisters and a brother to Lou. Theirs was ruled a fraudulent claim.

The attending physician at Lou's death sent the estate a bill for $1,700. Ankeny told the court he considered that a little high. He offered $400 instead, and the medic accepted.

Ankeny held an estate sale at Lou's home at 2102 East Madison Street. Her furnishings, jewelry and other personal effects netted $20,000 . . .

Translated into today's dollars, that would be $280,000 worth of personal property.

Ankeny enumerated the rooms and furnishing of the house at Third and Washington for the court. There were nine brass beds, two golden oak and one maple. They all had hair mattresses and French box springs. Those twelve beds made Lou's way in the world.

There was a saloon on the Third Avenue South side of the house and on the Washington Street South side a parlor, complete with over-stuffed furniture, live canaries, nude bronze statues of unspecified gender, lamps, China spittoons and a piano. Adjacent to the parlor was a dancing room. Elsewhere were the billiard room and the dining room, the latter with service for thirty. The house had a kitchen and a Turkish room with various artifacts from the Ottoman Empire, such as smoking equipment and lavish cushions and lamps.

Lou had a considerable amount of real estate: the three-story brick building at the corner of Third Avenue South and South Washington Street, the home on East Madison Street, three lots in Edmonds, three lots in Whatcom County, seventeen lots in King County, a block in Gloucester in Jefferson County, five lots in Tacoma.

The appraised value of this property was $86,000.

Because Lou had no heirs, the property went to support the common schools in King County.

So even after her death, Lou kept up her contributions to education.

A Woman of Means

Documents concerning the probate of her estate in King County Superior Court run to 150 pages. I'm taking the space here to enumerate Lou's material possessions because I want to show that she was a woman of means.

As I've mentioned, when I wrote about her twenty years ago, I did not have the complete story. I was aided in my research then by the recollections of two men who were making their way into our city's business establishment in Lou's day.

Henry Broderick, who built one of Seattle's most successful real estate companies, and Joshua Green, who was the most important figure in the Mosquito Fleet and later founder of one of our major banks, corroborated what I had heard about Lou's influence. And about her relationship with Jacob Furth.

They talked to me about her on the condition that their contribution to her story not be revealed until after their deaths.

As you can see, Lou's importance to Seattle has not been documented in the traditional ways.

More recently, I learned of an astonishing event not even hinted at in our history books. The flair Lou Graham showed in her part in this event must have been such that even the stolid Jacob Furth had to smile.

The story comes to me from Bob Crandall of Winthrop, Washington. Crandall promised his great uncle, whom he called "the old man," that he would keep the story alive.

"The old man" was John William "Saltwater Bill" Bullock. He came to Seattle from Alaska in the last decade of the nineteenth century with a sizeable poke and a desire to run for city council.

At that time any aspiring Seattle politician had to check in with one person. As Broderick told me: "It was a free country. Anybody who wanted to run for any office in the city government could do so if he chose. However, if he wanted to win, he cleared it with Jacob Furth before he threw his hat in."

When Bullock went to see Furth, the banker asked him where he had gotten his nickname.

Bullock told him that several cases of wine he had ordered for his small rest stop along the Klondike Trail had been dropped accidentally in the ocean en route. A bit of saltwater found its way into the wine bottles. Instead of throwing the wine away, Bullock said, he doubled the price and advertised it as the only saltwater wine in the world.

Furth advised Bullock to call himself "Saltwater Bill" in his council bid. He did, and he got himself elected during the Hiram Gill years.

That's when he heard the remarkable story of how Jacob Furth survived the 1893 panic.

It was a panic touched off when the Baring Brothers, principal backers of most of the country's enterprises, went bust. It was the bloody end for Tacoma, which until then had been the top dog on Puget Sound.

So Much for Brotherly Love

It was also a bad year for David Denny and the concept of brotherly love.

David didn't make it through the panic, but his brother Arthur did.

And there has been a certain amount of enmity among their respective descendants ever since.

While it was an economically sound move for Arthur to bring off a deficiency judgment against David, the action did not do much for family unity. Especially when the manager of the bank confessed on his deathbed to David's son: "We never should have done it."

Arthur attended David and Louisa's forty-second wedding anniversary the day before his bank took over all their assets.

Their daughter Emily Inez Denny was particularly bitter because her uncle's action robbed David of the burial site he owned in the cemetery that he gave to the city of Seattle.

The problem was, in all fairness to Arthur, pressure from some of the other principals at his and Dexter Horton's bank. He simply couldn't figure out how to avoid foreclosing on his brother.

Those were the days when the creditor took over the debtor's entire assets. Four years later the law was changed so that the creditor was entitled only to the amount of the mortgage.

It was the juxtaposition of the anniversary and the foreclosure that has provided the simmering resentment in the family ever since.

But everybody was a little jumpy during 1893.

People were nervous about their money.

Joshua Green told me that every banker in town knew the exact location of every single twenty-dollar gold piece.

Suddenly, there was a run on Jacob Furth's bank.

If he went under, everybody went under.

Our historians readily agree that Jacob Furth obtained $250,000 during the panic of 1893 and saved not only his bank but every other bank in town.

Adding Salt to Our History

And this is where Saltwater Bill comes in to supply the part of the story that's been missing for years.

Saltwater Bill realized that the story he knew to be true had absolutely no chance of getting into the history books when we were trying to make saints out of our ancestors.

So on repeated evenings with his worshipful nephew at his knees, he recounted one of the most colorful episodes in our past. He made the young Bob Crandall promise to remember the story he was telling and to make it available to historians.

One whole hell of a lot of Seattle's history has been expurgated, and of all the missing stories, Saltwater Bill's is the most important. It has to do with how Jacob Furth got that $250,000.

Between two hundred and three hundred people were lined up outside Jacob Furth's bank. These people all wanted to withdraw their funds.

When Lou Graham's satin-lined landau with the team of high-stepping horses pulled up in front of the bank, it was a familiar sight to everyone. The only curious thing was seeing the carriage during the week instead of on Sunday, as usual.

There, behind the top-hatted driver and the footman, was the bejeweled Lou.

All around Lou in the carriage were sacks of twenty-dollar gold pieces.

"Hi, boys," Lou called to a number of familiar faces in the line. "I just want you to know there are gold pieces in every one of these bags. They are all twenties. And they are all here to be deposited."

She threw a few samples into the crowd so they could be checked for authenticity.

Whereupon, driver and footman began hauling the loot out of the carriage and into the bank.

The unflappable Jacob Furth, with the customary Havana cigar clenched in his teeth, calmly watched the proceedings from his austere office.

By the time the massive deposit—perhaps 12,500 twenty-dollar gold pieces—had been counted and Lou had gotten her receipt, the line of panicked men had disappeared.

Jacob Furth's bank was saved.

I leave it to future students of Seattle history to authenticate all the details of this grand event.

Saltwater Bill was sure that on one day in 1893 the town's leading madam saved the town's leading bank. He was not sure of the exact amount Lou deposited. He knew only that it took quite some time to complete the transaction and that by the time Lou emerged from the bank, the scene on Pioneer Square was devoid of anything but the usual passersby.

I might speculate that the whole scene was Furth's concoction, a part he dreamed up for his leading lady. Lou had been Furth's friend and silent partner for five years in 1893. And Furth was just the kind of old fox who could have sneaked some of those twenties to Lou, whose flourishing establishment was only two blocks away. She then could have driven back with the great drama otherwise found only in B movies.

On the other hand, those were the days of the great madams throughout the United States. Two sisters in Chicago retired as millionaires after seven years in the trade.

Lou had a monopoly on parlor houses. It is certainly possible that in five years, with the prices she charged for wine and dinner and the interest from loans she made to bright and ambitious young men, she could have swung the $250,000 on her own.

According to Saltwater Bill, Furth was so pleased with Lou's performance or with her act of generosity that when an itinerant portrait artist stopped in Seattle, the banker commissioned a likeness of his benefactor. Saltwater Bill remembers seeing that portrait hanging in the lobby of Furth's bank for the rest of Lou's life.

I certainly hope that the portrait of Lou still exists and that someone will find it or come forward with it so that it can be hung once again where it belongs . . . in the lobby of one of Seattle's great financial institutions.

Lou Graham deserves that kind of acknowledgment.

After all, she gave her life for Seattle.

She died of syphilis.

She is buried in Lake View Cemetery, plot number 926, in the southeastern sector of the Capitol Hill burial ground, where Arthur Denny can look down on her. A flat, simple stone marks her place.

Oh, Frugal Us!

J ACOB FURTH'S OTHER PARTNER in the enterprise of building a great city on Puget Sound was James Jerome Hill, the most important citizen Seattle never had. Hill's Great Northern Railroad finally gave Seattle the transcontinental line that would make her Queen City of the Pacific.

James J. Hill and Jacob Furth were the two risk-takers who took hold of Seattle in her fifth decade (1890–1900).

They are two of today's least-honored historic figures.

They are two men who had one thing in common . . .

Money.

While Furth was learning English and saving half his $40-a-month salary, Hill was living free on Mississippi riverboats and looking for investments for the dollar a week his watchman's job paid. This was in a Minnesota town once called "Pig's Eye" and now called St. Paul.

Thrift, Jim Hill decided early, was the one quality that made life worthwhile.

This is the first time in my life I have summoned up enough spit to call him Jim Hill. When I was growing up, James Jerome Hill, the model for 135 books by a frustrated minister name of Horatio Alger, was shoved down my throat.

Jim Hill

My parents sang his virtues daily, and once a week at John Muir School in Rainier Valley, I was forced to emulate the great Mr. Hill. One of the lessons we got on Tuesday mornings at John Muir was a quote from the Hill:

> *If you want to know whether you are destined to be a success or a failure in life, you can easily find out. ARE YOU ABLE TO SAVE MONEY? IF NOT, DROP OUT. YOU WILL LOSE. You may think not, but you will lose as sure as you live. The seed of success is not in you.*

Every kid in every classroom in every school in Seattle was supposed to come to school on Tuesday morning with money to put in his savings account. It was Washington Mutual Savings Bank's "school savings" program. Teachers kept a supply of pennies on hand for the kids who dropped their money down the toilet or forgot to bring it or spent it on Horatio Alger stories or candybars.

We were afraid not to save money.

And when America is afraid, it makes jokes . . . like the one about the lady who heard that "frugal" meant to save. So when she fell in a lake she hollered, "Frugal me. Frugal me."

Back on Track

But we're getting a little off the track here, which is railroads.

And what Jacob Furth and Jim Hill had in common.

Which might have been two things . . .

Their judgment of men was the same: shrewd, swift and sure.

Ahhh, three things . . .

Once a judgment was made, they stuck to it with no regrets. And when they said yes to a deal, they did not throw all their chips into the pot . . . only enough to make the other guy work his tail off to do his fair share.

James Hill was the plain name his parents gave him when he was born on September 16, 1838, near Rockwood, Ontario. Until he was thirteen, he brooded over the fact that they had not named him Napoleon. Then he confronted his mother with his dissatisfaction.

At that time, Mrs. Hill was rather formidable herself. She and her son reached a compromise by inserting the name Jerome between James and Hill. Jerome was Napoleon Bonaparte's brother.

James Jerome Hill was blind in one eye as a result of a bow-and-arrow accident.

God, what if Hill's having one eye had taken hold the way his penchant for thrift did.

The American middle class would have consisted entirely of one-eyed men. Nobody would have been eligible to fight in World War I. They would have had to call it off.

Hmmm.

Even with one eye, Hill was a formidable physical foe. He was big and strong enough to throw a 300-pound rolltop desk out of his second-floor office. He didn't do that just for show. The building was burning, and he thought that tossing the desk out was the quickest way to save its contents.

Then there was the day he got real mad at Jay Gould. The story I like best about that incident is the one that has Hill charging into Gould's Western Union Building "fortress" in New York. This was the most protected private office in America. Gould was built like Casper Milquetoast, but other men had regretted ever lifting a hand against him.

Jim Hill tried something different.

He lifted Jay Gould and held him out his sixth-floor window.

While Mr. Gould was contemplating the pavement below, Mr. Hill requested that he call off his dogs in Washington, D.C. . . .

Those curs who were lobbying against the movement of Mr. Hill's railroad tracks through Montana.

Mr. Gould agreed. He was not even tempted to retaliate.

One Eye on the Orient

By 1889, Hill had been trying for thirty years to get to the Orient . . . at first on foot but later with transportation systems. He had the foresight to know that the future of enterprise lay across the Pacific. For a while he tried to get there as part of the Canadian Pacific Railroad Syndicate. He finally got so ticked off at Canadian government interference, he decided to build his transcontinental railroad south of the Canadian border in the United States, where the "lunatics had not as yet taken over the asylum." (Which, of course, they eventually did.)

Hill welded the St. Paul & Pacific Railroad and a few other odds and ends of transport systems into the St. Paul, Minneapolis & Manitoba. The St. Paul & Pacific had bravely started out for the Pacific Coast in the early 1870s and had foundered at Breckenridge, Minnesota, in the Panic of 1873.

Hill revived that transcontinental spirit. He renamed his railroad the Great Northern and was plowing through Montana en route to Puget Sound when he finally bought a copy of the 13-volume report compiled by Governor Isaac I. Stevens and paid for by the United States Congress. The report provided detailed information about a swath of land 250-miles wide following the general route taken by Lewis and Clark in the early 1800s and by Stevens half a century later.

Governor Stevens opined that the route had enough natural wealth to pay for construction of the railroad as it went along. There was a "lost" pass in the Rocky Mountains on the Marius River just waiting to be rediscovered at an elevation of only 5,000 feet.

Then there was Snoqualmie Pass in the Cascade Mountains at only 3,200 feet.

And just west of the lowest pass in the Cascades was the best town with the best harbor.

And as if he needed any further encouragement, Hill knew that his rival Northern Pacific had bypassed the best town in order to buy up Tacoma.

And if that wasn't quite enough, Hill got word that the best town with the best harbor had just been leveled by fire.

The secret of Jim Hill's phenomenal success as an empire builder lay in his system of espionage. Hill's espionage system would have made the CIA look like a Boy Scout troop. Hill always knew more about what was going on in the competition's camp than the head man of the competition.

Example: The Northern Pacific's agent in Helena was on Jim Hill's payroll.

Hill always knew more about the people he was about to do business with than the people knew about themselves.

Example: Two months after Seattle's fire, Hill sent his right hand man, Col. W. P. Clough, to the city. Clough had no difficulty finding members of the establishment for the simple reason that before going with Hill in the latter's westward expansion, he had been an officer of the Northern Pacific fighting Seattle's establishment tooth and toenail.

Clough reported to his boss in St. Paul that a fellow named Furth was the boss in Seattle.

Furth's banking operation was center stage after the fire. He was putting in those twelve-hour days, interviewing applicants, placing greater reliability on character than collateral. What it boiled down to was that the guys with the good ideas and hard-nosed business acumen got the loans.

For the other nine out of every ten, Furth suggested relocation in Tacoma. Finally Thomas Oakes, president of the Northern Pacific, protested, saying that the "freeloaders come to Tacoma while the fighters stay in Seattle and fight us."

Eventually Oakes decided to throw in his lot with the fighters. In 1890, when he was still president of the Northern Pacific, he sold out his real estate holdings in Tacoma and with $150,000 joined a syndicate that spent nearly half a million dollars buying land in Seattle.

Already Jim Hill was having a positive influence on Seattle's economy.

Seattle's Train Comes In

J IM HILL WAS AN EMPIRE BUILDER in every sense of the word. Before he was through, his empire would include the Great Northern, the Northern Pacific and the Chicago, Burlington & Quincy railroads, which would make him one of four men who controlled all of the railroads in the United States until the cartel was broken up by the Sherman Anti-Trust Law.

In 1889, the plucky little towns along Puget Sound were panting to be part of Hill's empire. Hill was proceeding steadily west. His style was not to select the next section for his track until he had completed the previous one. He would not have to announce his western terminus until he was nearly there. Everett, Fairhaven (now Bellingham) and Seattle all believed they had a chance.

During his scouting expedition to Seattle, W. P. Clough let it be known that his boss required certain things in a terminus, like freight yards and docking facilities at Smith Cove . . . a free and easy passage across the Seattle waterfront to more freight yards south of town.

After Clough returned to St. Paul, Thomas Burke, a Seattle attorney, took over the job of seeing how much Seattle was willing to give to Hill. Burke was well-acquainted with the fact that if you wanted to get things done in Seattle, you first checked in with Jacob Furth.

And one of the things he checked with Furth on was the open secret that Hill wanted to own and operate Seattle.

With or without Jacob Furth.

Hill had been in a race for some time with E. H. Harriman, who by 1889 had controlling interest in the Union Pacific. Harriman wanted his railroad to terminate in Seattle, coming up from Portland.

Harriman, who was every bit as cagey as Jim Hill, thoughtfully noted that the Vulcan Iron Works stood in a strategic spot about a mile south of Jackson Street. He had advance agents who were every bit as capable as those of Hill.

And what one of those agents did was have a little chat with the president of Vulcan Iron Works.

And who would that have been?

Ah, you knew . . .

Jacob Furth.

It was in 1887 that Furth organized Vulcan Iron Works. It was one of the earliest industries in Seattle.

An Impressive Introduction

Of course the ensuing proposal from Harriman's agent took place in Jacob Furth's office. Harriman's agent had a letter of introduction that would light up the eyes of any banker.

It was a check for $12,000,000.

What Harriman wanted in addition to the Vulcan Iron Works was an entry into the city of Seattle from Portland. He also thought it might be of strategic importance to keep the news of his wants from Thomas Burke.

What Mr. Harriman had in mind was a long string of properties on First Avenue South, Fourth Avenue South and Harbor Island.

Mr. Furth, who felt that he could oblige Mr. Harriman in this manner, summoned Frederick G. Struve, who happened to be a leading real estate figure. He was also Jacob Furth's son-in-law.

Struve assembled a group of his top real estate men. After briefing them quietly and intensively, Struve turned them loose to spend the twelve million. In one day, the money was gone and Harriman had a path for his entry into Seattle.

If Hill wanted Seattle, the Northern Pacific was not going to make it easy for him either. In 1890, the Northern Pacific bought the Seattle,

Lake Shore and Eastern, a regional line. Its depot was at Western and Columbia. It ran north to Ballard, then turned to run along the north shore of Lake Union and went on to Snoqualmie Falls. It had been founded in 1885 by, among others, Thomas Burke. Its most desirable feature was thirty feet of right-of-way to Railroad Avenue, a road along the waterfront designed to be used by all trains coming into Seattle.

Burke had tried to sell the S.L.S.&E. to Clough, who had just laughed and said the Great Northern was a railroad not a real estate promotion. The Great Northern eventually got sixty feet of right-of-way along Railroad Avenue, outside the Northern Pacific's portion.

During the last decade of the nineteenth century, railroad news dominated Seattle's papers. There were stories almost daily of plans for terminals, clashes, court battles.

Burke, acting on Hill's behalf, kept buying property south of Jackson. Furth was one of ten who coughed up a thousand bucks apiece to gather one obdurate landowner into the Hill fold.

Not one to alienate a potential power, Furth helped both Harriman and Hill make their way in Seattle.

The Northern Pacific tried to deal itself into control of the Seattle waterfront.

Hill kept laying track, coming steadily west.

I still don't know, and I haven't come across a likely explanation from anyone else, why Hill chose to go over Stevens, rather than Snoqualmie Pass. Snoqualmie was by all odds the shortest and best route.

Building the Great Northern track over Stevens Pass caused the worst railroad disaster in the nation's history. The pass was named for John Stevens, the engineer in whom Hill had more faith than anybody. The deaths of ninety-six people when an avalanche swept two trains into the canyon on March 1, 1910, must have haunted Hill for the rest of his life.

Maybe Hill was merely being cagey when he gave the nod to Stevens instead of Snoqualmie Pass. Choosing Snoqualmie would have sent a signal to Seattle that she was his destination. And don't think entrepreneurs in Seattle wouldn't have hung tough for better conditions.

With Stevens Pass, on the other hand, he could say, "I haven't made up my mind. I could go on to Bellingham Bay. I could take Everett."

Hill's going over Stevens Pass caused him to come into Seattle from the north. He had plans for a station on Jackson Street. Eventually, so that he could avoid the legal tangle that had developed along Railroad

Avenue, he would take City Engineer R.H. Thomson's advice and build a tunnel underneath downtown. That tunnel was built between 1902 and 1905.

A Low-key Entrance

Meanwhile, the Great Northern arrived in Seattle.

On January 7, 1893, the first Great Northern train on transcontinental track rolled into a humble depot at the foot of Columbia Street, carrying the construction superintendent's car and one passenger car. The final spike on the Great Northern was made of iron and driven in the presence of only the construction crew. The company had built a prodigious 556 miles of track in 1892 and hadn't time for any fancy gold spike ceremonies.

This was typical of Hill—get the job done first. Never mind the amenities.

Hill himself arrived two weeks later and said that in early June he would have a formal ceremony in Seattle and bring with him 300 men worth "a thousand million dollars" to see the great virgin territory in which investments would be so very worthwhile.

But before that could happen, Baring Brothers, principal backers of the Great Northern and most of the rest of the enterprises in the world, took its temporary nose-dive and Hill neglected to bring his party west. "That's all I'd need," Hill was quoted as saying, "a bunch of nervous millionaires on my hands."

The Great Northern's arrival in Seattle was by no means the end of the railroad wars.

The Northern Pacific kept trying to block Hill's plans to control railroading in Seattle. The Union Pacific rolled into town and built a large terminal on Jackson, next door to where Hill had planned to build his. Hill started quietly buying Northern Pacific stock.

By 1899 Hill had control of the Northern Pacific. He had offered to guarantee the interest on that railroad's mortgages. The Northern Pacific was financially strapped after making many mistakes, including its battle against Hill. Reorganization of the Northern Pacific lasted from 1896 until 1899.

I don't know what kind of thrill Hill felt when he took over the line that had tried to thwart him at every turn.

I imagine that he viewed the shift in Northern Pacific ownership as yet another lesson in thrift . . .

His real thrill probably came in 1896 . . .

That's when the first Japanese steamer arrived in Elliott Bay.

And the Great Northern was there to meet the Orient.

All Busted Up

*L*ET'S SEE WHAT JAMES JEROME HILL did for the city of Seattle. He built the shortest and most efficient transcontinental railroad in the United States to our door. He induced his pal Frederick Weyerhaeuser to purchase 900,000 acres of Northwest timberland; then he cut in half the cost of shipping lumber east. His railroad made Seattle the most attractive jumping off place for the Klondike and Nome gold rushes, which provided the government assay office with $200 million worth of gold bullion and set Seattle real estate values skyrocketing.

In the 1910 census, for the first time in its history, Seattle passed Portland in population. Tacoma was no longer a competitor.

Hill's agents covered every port in the Orient studying bills of lading to see what we might want to buy and what they could buy from us. He supplanted India cotton with cotton from Memphis. He underbid the British to provide Japan's burgeoning railroad system with track.

He increased trade through the Puget Sound Customs District by 4,000 percent and made Seattle the most important port on the Pacific Coast.

We did not repay him kindly. In fact, we took the lead with President Theodore Roosevelt in destroying his railroad empire.

In 1901, Hill had formed the Northern Securities Company to act as a holding company for the Great Northern, the Northern Pacific, the Burlington and others of his properties. This was one of the largest corporations in the world. It did not last long.

In 1902 Teddy Roosevelt brought suit under the Sherman Anti-Trust Law to break up the Northern Securities Company, which was said to be a "combination in restraint of trade."

The political reality for Teddy Roosevelt was a simple one. No vice president had succeeded to the presidency on his own after the death of the president.

Roosevelt needed a gimmick if he wanted to be elected.

It was called trust busting.

It worked because people were apprehensive about the concentration of so much wealth and power in the hands of so few.

Ironically, the mascot of the Great Northern Railroad was a stuffed mountain goat. Teddy Roosevelt turned it into a scapegoat.

The people, particularly populist Seattle, were with him.

In 1904 the Supreme Court ruled that the Northern Securities Company was in violation of the Sherman Anti-Trust Law.

James J. Hill made his last appearance in Seattle in 1909.

June 1, 1909, was a red-letter day in the city's history . . . a milestone in our progress toward the goal of becoming the Queen City of the Pacific. It marked the opening of the Alaska-Yukon-Pacific Exposition.

A crowd of 10,000 Seattle citizens straightened their shoulders as the squat, burly, bearded, bear-like Jim Hill walked up to the podium. They were awaiting a well-earned pat on the back.

What they should have done was bend over and present their posteriors for a well-aimed boot where it might do some good.

Jim Hill took aim in a figurative sense.

Hill could foresee that as a result of that Supreme Court ruling against him, five billion dollars in investments in the railroads of the United States would go elsewhere in the ensuing decade. The principal beneficiary of the high court's decision was the automotive industry . . . together with the nation's system of freeways. By 1919, our railroads were being referred to as "dinosaurs." They had been virtually been regulated out of existence.

In 1909, Hill was standing in front of a group of people who had turned on him. He remained polite through the opening words of his speech, but about two thirds of the way through, his outrage at what had happened burst through.

An Embarrassing Question

"Where," he asked, "are the men who used to match your mountains, like those who brought off the purchase of Alaska forty years ago when the issue was all but dead in Washington, D.C.? What happened to the spirit which rebuilt your city after it burned down twenty years ago?"

It is significant that he bore no malice to Jacob Furth for opening up Seattle to E. H. Harriman. That was the free enterprise system in operation.

Teddy Roosevelt had asked the boss of the Republican Party, Mark Hanna, what he thought of the Hill Lines. Hanna had responded that Jim Hill's railroads were the finest thing that ever had happened to the Pacific Northwest. Roosevelt left that meeting with Hanna and ordered him to break up the Hill Lines.

They would remain broken up—along with the city of Seattle—until 1970 . . . twenty years after we realized we had become a second-class city.

The citizens of Seattle on that day in 1909 had no idea they were celebrating the last of their glory days. They were congratulating themselves. They had seen their way toward honoring Jim Hill now that he had been taken down a peg. They planned to unveil a bronze bust of their humbled benefactor on the University of Washington campus, where the Alaska-Yukon-Pacific Exposition was held.

Hill, who had made the exposition possible in the first place, walked out on the unveiling of his bust. I don't know that anybody has ever wondered why.

I think Jacob Furth knew why.

The year after the exposition, Furth took a three-month trip to China to see what could be done about the city's backsliding into mediocrity. He returned with the realization that the best we could hope for was to remain on equal footing with the other major cities of the Pacific Coast . . .

Instead of being numero uno.

Thanks a Million

I F SEATTLE'S REIGN AS QUEEN CITY of the Pacific was about as short-lived as Jim Hill's Northern Securities Company, it was a good time nevertheless. In fact, at the beginning it was called the Gay Nineties.

While the big railroading interests were jostling to have their way downtown, local streetcar enterprises were springing up all over.

Electricity had just come on the scene, and electrified streetcars were the way to go. That is, once people got over their nervous curiosity.

They didn't know, for example, how piping electricity from Snoqualmie Falls to tideland would work. When Lowman and Hanford connected its steam printing plant (now in Seattle's Underground), the police cordoned off Pioneer Square to keep the crowds back. And only one man, the electrician, was allowed in to flip the switch.

When he emerged unscathed, the crowd broke into cheers.

The rich guys in town with any kind of sporting blood jumped into the streetcar business.

If you were Thomas Burke, you got together with some guys and bought up a bunch of land in and en route to a place called Ballard because William R. Ballard took the biggest plunge . . .

Or should we say bath?

The instigator of all this was Daniel H. Gilman, who was a perpetual plunger, along with John Leary who was bright enough not to take the entire plunge.

Notably absent from these early plungers was Jacob Furth.

Furth was as game as anybody when it came to taking a chance, but not until he had thought it through . . . and this one didn't look ripe to him.

It is of interest to note that J. J. McGilvra, who owned a bunch of property, did get into the streetcar business. He had a straight shot out Madison Street, and I suspect it was cable car all the way. McGilvra was another one who thought things through . . .

The wonderful part of the Gay Nineties devolved from the notion on the part of a lot of people that no matter what you did to it, the free enterprise system worked . . . but here was a case of too many cooks spoiling the broth.

There were fourteen separate streetcar lines in Seattle during the 1890s . . .

Thirteen, not counting McGilvra's.

Thirteen went bellyup.

A Run of Bad Luck

Thirteen may or may not be an unlucky number, but it sure was with Seattle. It initiated the bad luck that pursued this city for the next half century.

The panic of 1893 was too much for many of the streetcar barons, who were more interested in real estate promotion than anything else.

Naturally, they came running to Papa Furth, crying, "Save me. Save me."

So that's what Furth did.

He got everybody to sign on the dotted line that they would sell. And, with the options in his pocket to consolidate the lines into one huge system, he went to the prosperous Boston engineering firm of Stone and Webster.

In 1900 the Seattle Electric Company was formed, bringing all the streetcar lines together, plus the electric companies that supplied their power.

People had been paying a quarter to forty cents to get from one place to the next. After Furth's consolidation, anyone could go from one end of the city to the other for a nickel.

In 1902 Furth organized the Seattle and Tacoma Interurban Railway, which became the Puget Sound Electric Railway and which controlled the line between Seattle and Tacoma and owned the street rail systems of Tacoma and other towns on the sound.

The railway between Seattle and Tacoma had thirty-six miles of track and twelve cars. It also had a twelve-mile-long line to Renton, running four cars with hourly service.

The original Seattle Electric Company later became Puget Sound Traction, Light and Power and then Puget Sound Power and Light.

Furth gets all kinds of credit in our history books because he was selected by the state of Massachusetts to administer the million bucks that state raised for the victims of the San Francisco earthquake. When Massachusetts needed someone it could trust to be sure its relief money was properly spent, Jacob Furth was the man.

But our history books are not so proud of the million he raised in Massachusetts for a project much closer to home. He gets shot down for the capital he brought home for an integrated streetcar system.

The San Francisco million was a philanthropy.

The streetcar million gave the public-ownership people, a.k.a. "populists" and "progressives," the toehold to put their theories into actual practice for Seattle's experience with the "dark ages." And so soon after electrification, too.

A Proposal: Furth Place

Too Little, Too Late

*I*F JACOB FURTH hadn't sent out letters to forty men requesting contributions of $2,000 each, the Alaska-Yukon-Pacific Exposition would not be a high spot in Seattle history.

That self-congratulatory crowd wouldn't have had any place to gather that day to ignore Jim Hill's warning that their future was past.

Hill went home to Minnesota to write a book called *Highways of Progress*. In it he elaborated on the themes he had hinted at in the Alaska-Yukon-Pacific speech.

His philosophy was the one that helped our city realize, however briefly, her destiny. It is just as fundamental to Seattle today as it was eighty years ago, just after we had that glimpse of what it was like to be one of the nation's major cities.

The book begins:

> *Nations, like men, are travellers. Each one of them moves through history, toward what we call progress and a new life, or toward decay and death. As it is the first concern of every man to know that he is achieving something, advancing in material wealth, industrial power, intellectual strength and moral purpose, so it is vital to a nation to know that its years*

are milestones along the way of progress.

The methods suggested or adopted may be mistaken; may, and indeed often do, lead in the wrong direction. But the aspiration is true and it is constant. It searches always among policies, devices, inventions and systems for the few broad ways that lead to a real advance all along the line.

The great danger, to Hill, was the application of socialism as a method of coping with the human condition . . . a theory that if "literally applied, would destroy the vitality of society as an organic thing and establish a tyranny so universal and so minute as to make both the industrial and social life of man intolerable."

Jacob Furth understood Hill's message, but his era was ending in Seattle. The forces that would, some twenty years later, cause Postmaster James Farley to refer to the "forty-seven states . . . and the Soviet of Washington" were gaining ascendancy.

A Field Day at Furth's Expense

On September 27, 1912, Jacob Furth was meeting with someone in his office when a deputy sheriff served him with a warrant. The charge was conspiracy to violate the state's banking laws.

The private bank of one W. E. Schricker in La Conner had failed. It had less than $200,000 in assets and owed $378,766.91. Mr. Schricker blamed Jacob Furth for his problems . . . along with other officers of Furth's bank.

The day after Furth was arrested, the Seattle Star shrieked the news in an eight-column banner line in characters three inches deep.

The Star proceeded to have a field day with Furth. The paper printed a cartoon showing Furth, with a fat cigar in his mouth, sitting in a leather chair with his feet resting on a pillow on the floor. The deputy was depicted as a supplicant, begging Furth's pardon for the inconvenience of the warrant.

The Star labeled the banker "Jakey the Furth" and asked the snide question: "Why was J. S. Askew, a poor man, chucked into a jail cell following his arrest yesterday, while Jakey Furth, the traction king, was not even required to leave his comfortable office, when arrested on a charge of breaking state banking laws, yes, why?"

In the days that followed, the Star started calling him "King Jakey the Furth" in quotes like: "King Jakey the Furth says there's nothing to it and what the king says usually goes."

Furth did deny that he had aided Schricker in receiving deposits at the La Conner bank after he knew the institution was bankrupt. He said that he had known Schricker for over twenty years and had considered him a very conservative banker.

It was the one glaring mistake he had made in the thousands of fifteen-minute interviews.

Schricker had accused Furth of counseling him to continue taking in deposits even though he knew the bank was in danger of failing. The prosecuting attorney in the case went further. He accused Furth and three of his associates of keeping Schricker's doors open only long enough to be sure that he had paid notes due their bank, then letting him fail so that the farmers and other small depositors of the Skagit Valley would take the losses.

Until the Schricker bank had closed its doors, no one knew that Mr. Schricker had loaned $348,554.83 to the Fidalgo Lumber Company of Anacortes. Collection on those notes and overdrafts from Fidalgo would have nearly covered the bank's total liability.

However, there was something else no one knew at the time . . .

Schricker was a partner in Fidalgo Lumber.

Even though Schricker's business associations came out during the course of the trial, the jury found Furth guilty as charged. The verdict came on April 18, 1913. Superior Court Judge Ed. E. Hardin fined Furth $10,000.

Furth and his co-defendants appealed.

The case came before the state supreme court on December 18, 1914.

That court found that if Judge Hardin had known what he ought to have known, he would have thrown the case out before it ever came to trial . . .

Only that wasn't quite the wording used by the high court.

The decision was that the statutes under which Furth had been found guilty did not apply to him; his actions did not constitute a crime. Accordingly the court reversed the conviction and cleared Furth.

Only he never knew it.

He had died of cancer six months before the court cleared his name.

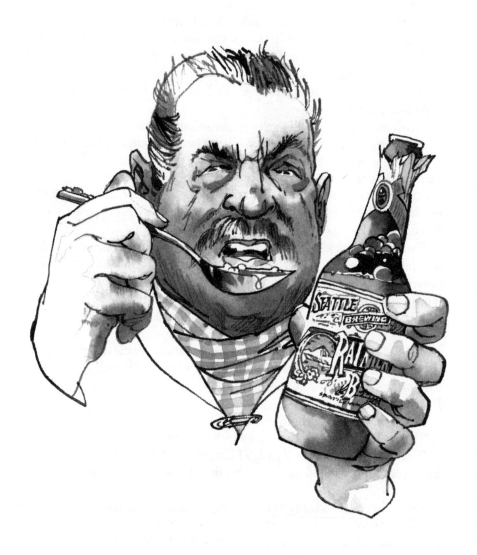

Cotterill

Furth Place

WHEN JACOB FURTH DIED, some of the strongest expressions of sorrow came from the people who had been his most vociferous opponents. The newspapers, in the unprecedented amount of space they devoted to his passing, reflected his contribution to the community.

If we can draw any conclusion from his contemporaries, we can say that they viewed Jacob Furth as the leading citizen of the Seattle of his day.

Yet, seventy-five years after his death, we have nothing to remind us of the contribution Furth made.

In the thirty years that he functioned as Seattle's most important citizen, here's what Furth did:

Eighty percent of the fresh water you drink today in King County you owe to Jacob Furth.

Furth gets the credit for providing $150 million, most of it without collateral, toward rebuilding the city after the great fire of June 6, 1889.

In the final analysis, it was Furth who brought us the Great Northern Railroad, which in turn provided us with the transportation system that brought us the Klondike Gold Rush and its contribution of $200 million.

During the panic of 1893 Furth saved not only his own bank from bankruptcy but also every other bank in town.

He brought us our public transportation system and reduced the cost of a fare to cross town from forty cents to a nickel and saved the bacon of the men who insisted on fourteen separate lines.

He would listen to anyone, no matter how small their problem. When a little boy came to Furth asking to borrow $2.50 to replace the skates he had just broken, Furth made the loan. The boy paid it back at ten cents a week.

"Every man should see that his design is wise and just," Furth believed, "and when that is ascertained he should pursue it resolutely, and not for one repulse or a hundred repulses could forego the purpose he has resolved to effect."

An Insufficient Monument

All these accomplishments, and the nearest thing we have to a monument to Jacob Furth, the most important man in Seattle's history after Doc Maynard, are the stubby I-beams sticking out of the back of the Pioneer Building.

If you stand in the alley between the Pioneer Building (600 First Avenue) and the Butler Garage (114 James) and if you look up to the sixth floor of the Pioneer Building, you will see the stubs of the I-beams that supported the city's first sky bridge.

They are a silent tribute to the artfulness and consummate skill with which Jacob Furth took Brat City and built Seattle into the metropolis of Puget Sound after the great fire.

The first sky bridge in the city of Seattle ran from the Pioneer Building to the sixth floor level of the Butler Hotel, whch was the most famous hotel in town in its time.

When the Pioneer Building was finished in 1892, Jacob Furth moved his bank offices into it.

As I mentioned in a previous chapter, he was a Bohemian gentleman who loved his family as much as he loved his poker. His weekly game was in the Butler Hotel.

He was apparently a very popular player. One story is that C. E. "Oakie" Farnsworth, a wealthy machinery man who sat at Furth's poker table every week, approached the banker with a check for

$10,000. Farnsworth had heard that Furth had made a New Year's resolution to give up poker.

When Furth inquired about the reason for the check, Farnsworth said: "If you will rescind your resolution, this check is yours."

"But why?"

"Because you are worth more to me than $10,000 every year, and I don't want you to quit the game."

Furth apparently did not give up poker. But sometimes these games went on all night. And there was the matter of embarrassment to either his wife or her friends should he appear in the lobby of the popular Butler Hotel en route to his morning shave in the basement of the Pioneer Building.

He solved that problem on his usual grand scale by creating the sky bridge.

I propose that Seattle matured enough now to recognize its connection to the Furth style of doing things.

Up to now, no public building, street, park or statue bears his name. We can fix that.

The Perfect Spot

For a century the little triangle at First and Yesler/James has been the crossroads of Seattle . . . bearing silent and unwitting witness that we stole this priceless piece of ground from the Indians in the original instance . . . and made it what it is today, the heart of the Queen City of the Pacific.

I refer, of course, to the drinking fountain decorated by the bust of Chief Seattle in the vain hope that mankind would turn from his sinful ways and consume less of what you see the habitues and sons of habitues tippling from wine bottles around the fountain.

Also among the objets d'art in this small triangle is the totem pole that members of the Seattle Chamber of Commerce on a goodwill mission to Alaska stole from an Indian reservation. When one of the habitues set fire to the original totem pole, destroying its usefulness as our city's centerpiece, we negotiated with that same Indian tribe to construct us another . . .

Which they gladly did . . .

Charging us double . . .

Once for the original, which we had stolen. And once for the new one.

They had learned the white man's ways.

The third piece of decoration in the triangle is our beloved pergola, restored at considerable expense by the United Parcel Service, the giant shipper that started as a small business under the sidewalk in Pioneer Square before the streets were raised.

We can stand under the pergola and look across Yesler at what we not so fondly refer to as the "sinking ship" garage, which must be retained as a sort of war memorial, a permanent reminder of what can happen when the owners of real estate in America conclude with that great philosophical observation:

"Nobody can tell me what I can do with my property."

Also across Yesler is the Olympic Block, the most historic piece of real estate in the city. It was on that ground that Doc Maynard named the infant city of Seattle. It is on that ground that the only new building to be erected in the Pioneer Square historic district in eighty years stands. That new building replaced a building that fell down because its owners wouldn't allow anybody to tell them what they could do with their property.

It seems to me that this little triangle, with its unique view of Seattle's past, is the perfect place. Groups of school kids could stand here and get a good dose of history.

The teaching of history, as you may know, is required by law in the state of Washington. In most instances, the ink, paper and facts are sterilized before anything goes to press . . . a process that caused one plucky pupil to write in the flyleaf of his history book: "If there is a flood, stand on this book. It's dry."

A city that would name a triangle after Jacob Furth would bequeath a lively history to its children.

The time has come to name the little triangle where he brought his wonders to our city "Furth Place."

Let George Do It

WHEN JAMES JEROME HILL was warning against the wrongheadedness of taking a system of preconceived notions and attempting to ram it down the throat of the human race, George F. Cotterill was getting out of the field of civil engineering, for which he was trained, and into social engineering, for which he was not trained.

While Hill was administering his kick to Seattle's posterior at the Alaska-Yukon-Pacific Exposition, a system of morality and economics that substantively reflected Cotterill's social notions was becoming a major part of Washington jurisprudence.

Cotterill had two items on his social agenda: public ownership of utilities and prohibition of the consumption of alcoholic beverages.

Everyone knows that if the people are going to run anything, they had better be sober.

And everybody knows that the way to keep people from drinking is to pass a law against alcohol.

Cotterill arrived in Seattle in 1885 at the age of 25.

He could see right off that he had God's work cut out for him. The fellow who ran the town, Jacob Furth, had a silent partner named Lou Graham, who was a practitioner of the world's oldest profession.

This was bad, but it was also symptomatic of the moral decay eating away at the entire nation. Grover Cleveland was president, and the popular chant about an illegitimate son asking after his father was: "Ma, Ma, where's my pa? He's in the White House. Ha. Ha. Ha."

A short way to describe George Cotterill would be to call him the thin man. He was thin when he graduated as the valedictorian from his high school at the age of 15. And he certainly was thin when at the age of 18 in Kalama he had to make the first great basic decision of his life. He was down to his last twenty-five cents. It would buy a good dinner or lodging for the night.

George picked the hotel room.

A great deal of what happened in Seattle after we decided to turn things over to George hinged on his resemblance to a bean pole.

Food meant little to him.

He would have called it sustenance.

Drink was an evil.

According to the Argus, a doctor prescribed beer to relax George's nervous system . . . but it didn't work.

"Are you drinking beer?" the good doctor asked.

"Absolutely."

"How much?"

"One tablespoon three times a day after meals."

A Career Built on Water

George made his reputation on water.

And for awhile it seemed that was the only liquid anyone in the state of Washington would be allowed to drink.

George had a number of notions about how man could be freed from the grasp of sin. But at first he couldn't do much with them. He was trudging about in the wilds of Kitsap County laying out Port Orchard.

Then he went to work for R. H. Thomson as his assistant city engineer.

Thomson was pushing for that gravity-flow water system. It would cost $1.25 million.

Cotterill launched his political career by taking the credit for a gimmick called revenue bonds. A municipal corporation could issue the bonds to build the water system, pledging future revenue from the new system.

That way Seattle could have its water system and not exceed its debt limit, the one imposed on the city by general obligation bonds.

Pure clean water from the Cedar River.

Coursing through a system owned by the people.

And not costing them anything up front.

That's the stuff political futures are made of.

A lady living in Ballard went down to the Ballard City Hall carrying a pail of worms she had collected just by running the water out of her kitchen faucet. So Ballard stopped being a city unto itself and became part of the city of Seattle.

You didn't get worms in your water when you joined Seattle . . . which a lot of people with worms did. Worms more than doubled the Seattle population between 1900 and 1910.

And gave George Cotterill even more clout.

In 1895 he started pointing out to that growing population that he personally had invented the concept of the revenue bond in order to bring water to the people.

"Normally," George would say, "the idea of a revenue bond is something you might expect a private banker to come up with. But here am I, a servant of the people, thinking up the idea of the revenue bond . . . making great public works like the municipally owned Seattle Water Department the great institution for good that it is . . . proving once and for all that you don't need the profit motive to come up with ideas for the good of the people."

Of course, it wasn't until after old George had done all of his damage that the history of the Seattle Water Department, written by a little old lady in tennis shoes, put a new light on the invention of the revenue bond.

People found out then that revenue bonds weren't the invention of George F. Cotterill at all.

They were invented by some Eastern bankers.

Who were in it for the buck.

If It's Fun, It's Illegal

George had repeated his lie so many times that maybe he started believing it himself. Part of his genius was that he got everyone believing it.

In 1906 he was elected to the state senate.

In 1909 he used his considerable persuasive abilities to get his fellow legislators to pass laws making anything that was any fun illegal.

Yes, the Blue Laws were the result when we started letting George do it.

I suppose the surgeon general would go along with George's ideas on smoking. George's legislature passed a law fining anyone $250 if he was caught with so much as a cigarette paper in his possession.

Under that law one fervent judge fined a man $20 for having what appeared to be nicotine stains on his fingers.

This was George F. Cotterill's first major triumph.

As we moved into our seventh decade (1910–1920), George was beating the devil. No question about it . . . he was sending that devil packing, red suit, horns, temptation and all . . . forked tail tucked between his legs.

A Dream Runs Dry

ALTHOUGH HE WAS our mayor for only one term (1912-1914), Seattle's sorry seventh decade (1910–1920) belongs to George Cotterill. He was the next in line after Jacob Furth in guiding the city's destiny.

But where Furth ushered us into first place among cities, Cotterill steered us straight into the mire of public morality.

There were George Cotterills all over the Pacific Northwest in the early 1900s.

Hell, they were all over the United States.

But Mr. Cotterill was Seattle's.

He took his text from that great quote of Sir Galahad: "My strength is as the strength of ten ... because my heart is pure."

He represented the high point of the progressive movement in Seattle.

He knew better than other people what was good for them.

And he knew that all you had to do to make them happy was to legislate sin out of existence.

Cotterill proposed a "reign of the people."

To begin with, he believed that Jim Hill was nothing but a goddamn crook who was bleeding the common man dry.

It cost only $2 to run a railroad, but Hill charged "the people" $4. Wow.

All you had to do was turn the railroads over to "the people" and you would save 50 percent.

This was like believing you could fix the way a watch ticked by removing the main spring.

George started referring to the Great Northern as the road that obstructed progressivism.

He also campaigned for years on the moral value of municipal ownership of our streetcar system.

The people would take over the control of all public utilities because it was morally right for the people to own all public utilities.

It was morally right for the public to take over the ownership of the streetcar system that Mr. Furth had struggled to consolidate.

It was a lot like stepping on a dog's tail and then wondering why he was trying to bite you.

Mr. Cotterill was not a bad engineer. In fact, he was a real stem-winder . . . as long as somebody else told him what to do. When they told him to go lay out Port Orchard or Laurelhurst or Mount Baker, he went and laid out Port Orchard and Laurelhurst and Mount Baker. When they told him to lay out bicycle paths to get started on our system of boulevards, he laid out bicycle paths that could be turned into boulevards. That's what he did . . .

Or the piers in our front yard: "Aim 'em at Magnolia Bluff."

George aimed 'em at Magnolia Bluff.

George was a hell of an engineer.

He got so good at surveying, he started to believe he could think.

George Gets His Way

How to further describe one of our most interesting mayors?

If he was in an airplane and three of the four engines broke down, he would most likely say: "I hope that fourth engine keeps running, or we'll be stuck up here all night."

Here's part of George's address to the Seattle City Council in 1913 when, as mayor, he had the privilege of giving an annual message to that body:

The liquor traffic aggravates and increases every evil which it does not directly create. On the ledger of individual or community progress, it is altogether and always a liability. It inflicts public and private injury without a suggestion of benefit save to the gratification of the inhuman greed of those who are willing to coin manhood into money . . .

What was all that about?

He was persuading the city council to pass an ordinance that would prohibit a man from taking a glass of wine with his dinner in any restaurant where women and children were present. It was a law that exhilarated Mr. Cotterill.

But it sure was tough on the restaurant industry . . .

For the next thirty years . . .

During which time the fine old restaurants in Seattle died like flies. No new dining spot with the accommodations we have come to expect in our cosmopolitan city opened its doors.

But that city council action was not the pinnacle of George's political career.

The pinnacle came the next year in 1914 when he was 49.

That was the year that Washington voted in Prohibition for the whole state.

When George was a state senator, he had pushed through a law known as "local option," which left the decision whether to be wet or dry up to individual counties. Over a period of several years, various counties eliminated the manufacture and sale of alcoholic beverages . . . until a majority of the counties were thus committed. Then they held a vote, and the whole state went dry.

The local option tactic has its parallel today among anti-abortionists, who have pledged to win their fight to save the lives of the unborn "doctor by doctor, hospital by hospital and county by county."

George had the unusual experience of seeing what would happen when his dreams came true.

His dream had whispered to him that a law against liquor would bring morality to public office. Men and women would stop spending money on alcohol and would buy baby shoes and groceries instead.

Is that what happened, George?

The way I hear it what once had been a loosely controlled business went underground . . . and above ground and in ships at sea. The free enterprise system prevailed. Nobody knew for absolute sure, but the people in charge of busting them up estimated that there were 10,000 stills operating in the state of Washington.

Seattle served as the entryway for a flood of booze from Canada.

A national humor magazine showed a cartoon of a billboard for Canada Dry ginger ale . . . With the slogan "Drink Canada Dry" . . . and a blowsy drunk leaning against a lamp post and slurring: "It can't be done."

The leading importer of wet goods from Canada initiated a boat building program that eventually brought the hydroplane gold cup to our city. Commenting on pursuit by the anti-alcohol unit of the federal government, our importer opined: "The Feds are so slow they couldn't catch a cold."

The town's bootleggers held a convention in one of our leading hotels to set standards for the 300 speakeasies that freely plied their trade.

George Loses His Way

George Cotterill was a one-term mayor and had to watch while his successor Hiram Gill formed dry squads that made two of their first raids on the homes of William E. Boeing, the man who started the company all of us are familiar with today . . . and of David E. Skinner.

Mr. Skinner's name is not so well known as that of Mr. Boeing, until you put it together with the Alaska Steamship Company.

Skinner's Alaska Steamship Company helped to create the modern container, that product of which there are about eighty million now carrying goods around the world.

Prior to the passage of the Prohibition law in the state of Washington —some six years ahead of the national version—Mr. Boeing and Mr. Skinner had spent years of their time and a fortune in money building up wine cellars worthy of the mansions that housed them.

They did not appreciate having those dry squad axes applied to their homes and their wine cellars.

They did not stand by while the dry squad smashed their precious collections and think appreciatively of the good that Mr. Cotterill's efforts had created.

At least Mr. Boeing and Mr. Skinner didn't move out of town. Their wives liked Seattle and soothed them into staying.

And they started a movement to repeal the national Prohibition law . . .

Before it was even passed.

When the day of that repeal did come, it was Miss Augusta Ware Webb Trimble who had organized her sisters in the state of Washington into the Women's Organization for National Prohibition Reform. Miss Trimble's blood was so blue they used it to color the field in which the stars of the American flag were set. What we now call Blake Island used to be called Trimble Island.

On Miss Trimble's advisory committee was none other than Mrs. William E. Boeing.

George Cotterill lived to see the repeal of his dry dream.

What happened in the 1920s was not the Utopia that he and others like him had envisioned.

While Prohibition was in effect, the number of persons who died of an illness called alcoholism increased.

We went through the whole drill without even realizing that it was not a moral problem at all. It was physical.

Count Your Blethens

*T*HE SELF-PROCLAIMED most moral mayor in Seattle's history had some trouble making himself appreciated and understood. People simply didn't respond well to what was good for them. And one of the people who disappointed George Cotterill was Colonel Alden Blethen, publisher of the Seattle Times.

Colonel Blethen is reputed to have had something of a temper. He wore heavy gold rings on his fingers ... and there was a valley of splintered wood along the top of his desk ...

Put there on those occasions when the only way he could express his anger was by pounding on that hapless piece of furniture.

The colonel also tore his telephone from the wall so regularly that a repairman was posted on permanent standby.

Now all that Mayor Cotterill did was throw a platoon of policemen around the perimeter of the Times the day the colonel printed something that the mayor did not consider the kind of news that should be read during the reign of the people.

The colonel got mad. He started pounding the desktop. The telephone repairman had to be summoned.

This was in the middle of 1913 during a civic festival called Potlatch

Days. The colonel's paper had run a story implying that the visiting secretary of the Navy had insulted the mayor. The story also inflamed people against certain leftist elements.

Cotterill knew what to do to keep things from getting out of hand. First he ordered all the saloons closed.

Then he told the colonel he could not publish his paper again until Potlatch Days were over.

A superior court judge had to hold an emergency session on a Saturday morning to tell George he was out of line.

The second Colonel Blethen was a little bit friendlier to Cotterill's ideas.

Clarance took over the Times when his father died in 1915.

On March 24, 1917, an article he wrote appeared in Colliers, the national weekly. It was entitled "One Year Dry. Does Prohibition Mean Less Business? Washington's Answer."

Blethen explained he had been a long-time wet but now realized his error. He said habitues of the Skid Road were buying shoes instead of booze and going to the movies instead of saloons.

Prosperity had come to Seattle and Blethen gave the credit to Prohibition. He seemed to ignore the possibility that World War I and the opening of the Panama Canal were factors.

One of the things about the second Colonel Blethen was that his butler, George Baldwin, would travel to Vancouver, B.C., doubling as the steward of his yacht. There Baldwin bought ship's stores, including cases of scotch, bourbon, gin and the like, charged among the other groceries to the colonel's account. Before the yacht returned to the United States, the colonel ordered that all alcoholic beverages on board be emptied except for one stout highball for the customs official and one for the colonel.

"This," the colonel would announce jovially on the afterdeck as the two men drank a toast, "is the last drink on board."

The shaking English butler Baldwin knew better.

Below decks were several cases of the finest Canadian whiskey . . . which Baldwin would sell to the colonel at bootleg prices once they got the stuff safely in the colonel's wine cellar.

Baldwin always said the colonel got the best . . .

Even if the best cost a little more in the United States than in Canada.

Baldwin always kept his bags packed for a fast flight back to England.

Mrs. Blethen never trusted him.

But the colonel knew that good English butlers were hard to find.

What are a few peculations on the part of the man who snaps on your garters seven days a week?

Dragon's Teeth

Dragon's Teeth

ONE OF THE THINGS we should have learned during the '30s and '40s was that there are no cast iron ass protectors. We probably didn't, but maybe history can help us sort it out.

What you hear now about the decade of the '30s is the terrible Depression. Franklin Delano Roosevelt came riding in on a white charger and saved us. He wouldn't have ridden very far if the "kept" press, as it is so often disparagingly known among the cognoscenti (the people who don't have to look up that word to know what it means), had told the American voters a little more about him.

Roosevelt had his function. He conned us into believing that the only thing we have to fear is fear itself. He also closed down the banks so we couldn't express any fear in the economic system. And then he proceeded to get out the nation's checkbook and go on a spending spree.

There were about twelve million unemployed and they had to eat. I kid you not.

They were really intent on eating.

Governor Clarence D. Martin, a Republican in Democratic clothing, put it bluntly when he said it was much cheaper to feed the hungry than to fight them.

The Republicans crossed over in the primary and voted for Martin, or we would have ended up with a guy who had his name legally changed to Radio Speaker. John C. "Radio Speaker" Stevenson was wanted by various authorities in New York and had to avoid that state on his trips to the East.

We had a lot of fuzzy-headed people in Seattle in those days, and they wanted us to turn to communism, under which capital couldn't exploit labor and everybody had a job. You got about an equal portion of that stuff on the University of Washington campus and the Skid Road, where there was a soap box on every corner and a different theory on how to solve our problems.

Joseph Stalin was running Russia, and he didn't tell nobody nothin'.

The people who disagreed with him found themselves bundled off to Siberia, or shot or starved. The number who died would have cut quite a hole in our unemployment rate. Nobody really knew the score until Nikita Krushchev blew the whistle on his boss twenty years later.

Tough Times for the Colonel

Times were tough for the Times, too.

Colonel Clarance B. Blethen had to sell his yacht. The Canim had been designed by naval architect Ted Geary and built for $150,000. In 1931, the colonel had to sell it for $47,500, to one of the few people in the United States who could afford to pay even that much, straight-faced comedian Buster Keaton.

To keep his newspaper alive, the colonel had to make a deal with the Ridder Brothers. He could continue as a publisher only so long as the paper made a profit.

If the colonel didn't swim, he was sunk.

And there was no yacht to come along and scoop him out of the water.

But he did what he had to do and retained control.

But what else was new back in the '30s?

Philip G. Johnson was new.

Well, not exactly new.

He was an engineering graduate of the University of Washington who went to work for William E. Boeing, who had that little company named after him. William E. Boeing had no use for Franklin D. Roosevelt and what he was doing to the Boeing Company.

So Boeing blew his cork and turned the operation of his company over to Philip G. Johnson, a roly-poly and enthusiastic man who simply didn't believe the generals and other graduates of military schools when they said you couldn't build a big bomber that would fly faster than a balloon.

He was one of our "the hell I can't" people if ever there was one.

He had a pair of sharp blue eyes that saw through the phonies fast.

And what is more, he had that jovial genius to persuade other men that hell if they couldn't, too.

Under his enthusiasms various people stuck their necks out to prove that airplanes didn't necessarily have to continue in a spin once they started . . . that the leading edge of the wing could be de-iced . . . that the trailing edge could free you of static . . . that people could talk to one another from air to ground and back . . . that automatic pilots could work . . .

That a thirty-ton airplane could fly 2,000 pounds of bombs 5,000 miles.

That United Airlines, started by the Boeing Company, could fly mail cheaper than the government could.

And that's where the American way came into play.

Same Trick, Different Roosevelt

A newspaper columnist persuaded Roosevelt that he could get publicity and votes if he did the same to Philip Johnson that his old cousin Teddy had done to James Hill.

And, by God, it worked!

They broke a scandal on the head of Phil Johnson, stating that he had been stealing the people blind with the airmail contracts. Boeing and United Airlines were accused of conspiring to defraud the public.

Roosevelt banished Phil Johnson from working in the airplane business in the United States.

Roosevelt turned the airmail business over to the United States Army . . .

And twelve pilots were killed in the two months that the U.S. Army tried to deliver the mail and before public outcry gave the job back to United Airlines (and, of course, others) . . .

Who carried the mail for less than half of what it was costing the government.

The genial Franklin D. you heard on the radio could be the venal Franklin D.

Johnson went to Canada and put together TransCanada Airlines.

Then, all of a sudden, we needed long-range bombers in a hell of a hurry.

FDR quietly let Johnson's banishment lapse . . .

Proving that even U.S. presidents could use a few erasers on their pencils.

Johnson returned to Seattle where he engineered the construction of the B-17 and B-29 bombers.

A copy editor, long forgotten in the mists of history, put the caption "Dragon's Teeth" with a newspaper photograph of a row of Flying Fortresses. When the picture was taken, the planes were facing the administration building at the Boeing Company. Their tails certainly did resemble dragon's teeth.

If you think the planes arriving and leaving Seattle today make a racket, think of what it was like in Germany during World War II with those bombers day and night . . .

The dragon's teeth from Seattle.

A Thirst for Life

ONCE TAINTED by the deadly forces of righteousness, most cities wither and die . . . after all, they are only human. Righteousness, like AIDS, immobilizes the immune systems and death can come from any variety of causes.

Seattle, for instance, was exposed to that deadly virus of efficiency administered in the original instance when Arthur B. Langlie was mayor in the 1940s and ruthlessly rooted out our cable cars.

Then Langlie went on to become governor and to level the full force of that office against laughter.

He couldn't have done it without the backing of the people in the "society," who had brought about the repeal of Prohibition. They reasoned, for instance, that they had brought off the very difficult task of repeal and now they should reap the benefits.

The common man was permitted his mead parlors — notoriously known as taverns, where the law required that people passing by on the streets could look in the big window and see what kind of monkey business was going on inside and report it to the police.

Singing, of course, was prohibited.

It was all right to ingest the mead if it had a low enough alcohol content.

It was okay to drink beer.

But not to have fun.

Then along came the traveling man.

Traveling men had been here before. They were always a boon to the economy. They had been lured here by the Klondike Gold Rush in the 1890s. Then they could wear any kind of gear they wanted, although the businessmen who stayed here to mine the miners preferred that they buy their outfits in Seattle.

The new breed of traveling men wore khaki clothes provided by the United States government, which finally had found out that there was such a thing as the Great Circle Route. And Seattle was the closest city to Tokyo.

That's where Hirohito was.

And that's where the guys were going.

To give you some kind of an idea of the impact of that crowd . . .

A young man named Sam Israel got the contract for repairing the shoes of the traveling men.

Now Sam owns a big chunk of Pioneer Square.

The city's birthplace.

Thousands of traveling men who were en route to meet Hirohito in Japan found the original sorting job was done by the rain. We, of course, take the position that there is no rain in hell and that's your alternative if you don't like it here.

We don't want just anybody.

The railroads, the poor old goddamn busted up railroads, saved our bacon again by delivering the materiel of war in greater quantity and at less cost than ever. They carried ten times as much freight as they did passengers and they learned the big lesson that Jim Hill had been trying to tell them all along.

Freight doesn't squawk to the Justice Department.

Freight doesn't really squawk to anybody.

And, in America, that's where the money is.

Freight.

We showed pictures of dancing girls to the traveling men as they came and went on the big ships, and they thought they might be able to have fun here. They didn't know you had to belong to a private club to drink real booze. But there were willing ladies, called "B girls" because they hung around the mead parlors. And penicillin had come in by then and helped sort the good from the bad.

The people who survived the rain and the B girls and wanted to come back were the kind of people we wanted.

What About When the Sun Goes Down?

In 1948, a reporter from a national magazine was being shown the wonders of our geographic features. "Yeah," he said, "but what do you do when the sun goes down?"

A century earlier Doc Maynard had done what he needed to do to provide night-time entertainment in competition with the other little towns on Puget Sound. The others rolled up their sidewalks when the sun went down. But Seattle was the place to come for fun as well as business.

In 1948 we were in competition with the rest of the world, not just with the struggling little towns on the Sound.

If you didn't belong to a private club, you stayed in your hotel room and drank from a bottle. No first-class restaurant had started up for the past thirty years.

It was time to bring Seattle to life again.

And the man to do it was Eddie Carlson.

He was to Seattle, as the city neared its hundredth birthday, what Doc Maynard and Jacob Furth had been. He was the risk-taker with the vision and the luck to pull us out of the after-dark dark ages: to create the setting for new restaurants and legitimate entertainment.

The dour Governor Langlie knew Eddie Carlson. They were friends and had, in fact, been fraternity brothers at the University of Washington. Langlie informed his friend that he had no chance of getting liquor by the drink through the legislature. And even if he beat the odds and got such a bill through, his old pal fraternity brother the governor would veto it.

Eddie was working for Western Hotels at the time, which later became Westin International and is now Westin Hotels and Resorts. He had the support of the hotel and restaurant industry. He decided that the only way to get liquor by the drink was through an initiative . . .

One of the weapons that George Cotterill had created in order to dry up the state.

No wonder politicians drink.

The Two Percent Solution

Eddie rounded up a committee called Common Sense Control and got Henry Broderick to serve as chairman, for the "touch of respectability that we desperately needed," Eddie told me in an interview in 1985.

They started working to get the people to vote yes on Initiative 171.

They were up against not only the lunatics who thought you could keep people from drinking by passing laws against it but also the private clubs, one of the most powerful lobbies in the state.

The private clubs liked having control of the liquor trade. They did not want to give up their monopoly. They used a high-minded argument in defense of their restraint of trade.

The attitude that the private clubs endorsed was pretty well summed up by Elmer Todd, president of the Seattle Times, when Broderick and Carlson paid a visit to his office to determine what the paper's editorial position would be on Initiative 171.

As Carlson described Todd's reaction:

> *The upshot of it was that Mr. Todd said: 'I understand this is going be kind of a close election. I don't think liquor by the drink is in the best interests of the state. I think the club view takes care of these people who ought to be given the opportunity to drink. And it was okay, we've got it, but I'm not sure it should be made available to the masses. They may abuse it.'*

Despite Todd's views, the Times took no position on the issue. Carlson attributed that silence to the friendship between Todd and Broderick.

The private club position that only the elite could hold their liquor was put to a vote of the masses.

The entire nation was surprised by the results of that November 4, 1948, election. Truman beat Dewey.

And in the state of Washington, the masses opted for liquor by the drink. It was 51 percent for and 49 percent against.

That two percent solution meant Seattle could get back on track again to becoming Queen City of the Pacific.

Seattle Takes to the Air

THE YEAR 1948 was a remarkable one in Seattle for another reason. That's the year William Allen won, and the Aero Mechanics Union lost.

The issues were simple. The union wanted a closed shop. The Boeing Company wanted optional union membership for its employees.

The union wanted strict seniority. The company wanted more flexibility.

Bill Allen had taken over the leadership of Boeing in 1945, after serving as legal counsel to the firm for twenty years. He had drawn up the first "cost plus a fixed fee" contract, which became the model for wartime government work.

Allen was the one who persuaded the chairman of the board to bring Philip Johnson back from exile to lead Boeing's war effort. Then in 1944 Johnson died suddenly. Boeing was without a chief executive officer for nearly a year.

Allen was leading the committee searching for someone to take Johnson's place.

Finally, the board prevailed upon him to look in the mirror.

He talked it over with his wife. He told her he would have to work a little harder and would be bringing home a bit more money . . .

She gave him her blessing . . .

So Bill Allen became the new Boeing CEO.

Right away he faced cancellation of $1.5 billion in wartime contracts. He had to lay off 38,000 people.

Then the Aero Mechanics walked out. The 14,000 union members were out for 144 bitter days. Allen refused to bargain with them, claiming their strike was illegal under the terms of their contract.

Allen allowed the Teamster leader Dave Beck in to reorganize the union.

The Aero Mechanics went back to work, and Allen started to move the Boeing Company into the jet age.

In the early 1950s he committed $20 million to development of the 707, the first U.S. jet airliner. There were no customers lined up waiting for it. It was the biggest risk Bill Allen had taken so far.

The commercial airlines were not particularly eager to buy jets, since they had just spent millions updating their fleets of prop-driven planes.

But Allen's 707 was irresistible and made Boeing the leader in the peacetime commercial market, as it had been in the wartime military market.

Allen never stopped taking risks.

In 1975 Fortune magazine named him to the "Business Leaders Hall of Fame," one of nineteen inductees for all of American history. Part of the magazine's commentary on Allen was that he "led the Boeing company into some of the greatest gambles in U.S. business history because he had no riskless options."

He knew he was taking risks . . .

He didn't flinch . . .

And gambled right up until the day he cleaned out his desk.

When Allen retired from Boeing, he had just spent $1 billion developing the 747. There were no customers for that plane either.

Can you imagine the skies today without that hump-backed whale of an airplane?

Quick Like a Bullitt

Oh yes, there was one more signal event of 1948.

That was the first television broadcast in Seattle. It was Thanksgiving Day, and the program was a high school football game.

A fellow by the name of P.K. Leberman had seen the potential of the new medium and had acquired a license for Channel 5 from the federal government. He set up his offices in an old butcher shop.

Nobody much noticed his grand opening . . .

Except for Dorothy Bullitt . . .

She sent flowers.

She knew what she was doing when she sent flowers. She just didn't know she was opening Seattle's second century celebration.

But the ghosts of our past knew.

For instance, Louisa Boren knew.

It was nearly a hundred years after Arthur Denny had told Louisa Boren, "You can't do that," and Louisa responded with something like, "The hell I can't."

No one paid much attention to the new television station. Those who were aware of it considered it a venture absolutely destined for failure. Only 6,000 people in town had television sets. The broadcast hours were from 4 to 10 p.m.

Soft-spoken, ladylike Dorothy Bullitt was the only human being to send a congratulatory bouquet to the opening. Against all advice from her male economic advisers, Dorothy was intrigued by the idea of television. She admired anyone with the courage to start up a station.

When Leberman got an offer he couldn't refuse to move east and wanted to unload his broadcast hobby, the first person he thought of was Dorothy Bullitt.

A Woman of Means

Not only had she sent flowers, but she also had resources.

She was the daughter of C. D. and Harriet Overton Stimson, who had moved from the Midwest to Seattle in 1889.

The way one of Dorothy Bullitt's daughters puts it, C. D. came to Seattle to cut down the trees and Harriet came to plant them; he came to settle and she came to civilize.

He bought an old sawmill in Ballard and built the Stimson Mill Company. She was the founder of the Seattle Symphony Orchestra.

Dorothy was born in a house on Queen Anne Hill in 1892.

Dorothy Stimson married a transplanted Southern Democrat named Scott Bullitt, whose passion was politics. Shortly before he was to put Franklin Roosevelt's name in nomination at the 1932 national convention, he died of cancer of the liver. Dorothy took his place at the convention.

She was 40 years old and had three children at home.

Those were the days when the woman's traditional role was to have the idea, like Mrs. Thomas Kane who made her husband president of the University of Washington when she could have made some other man president of the United States.

Dorothy had no man to turn to.

Her father had died in 1929, and her only brother Thomas in 1931.

She was in charge of a rather large estate.

But she declined Leberman's offer of a little television station.

She had formed KING Broadcasting in 1947 and bought a radio station. She was intrigued by television but not quite ready to take the plunge.

Leberman offered his television station to KIRO and KOMO radio. They turned him down, too.

Then he threw in an FM radio station as part of the deal.

Suddenly, Marshall Field of Chicago was interested. Field's representatives came to Seattle to see if they couldn't pick up a bargain.

You know the song in Wizard of Oz about the yellow brick road?

Our Dorothy didn't follow it.

She built it.

She changed her mind about Leberman's offer and took the biggest chance of her life. She paid $375,000 for the Northwest's first television station.

Marshall Field's agents went back to Chicago wondering what had happened. They had been authorized to spend $500,000 to acquire the station.

But they hadn't sent flowers.

Dorothy's gamble paid off.

Because of transmittal problems, the government put a freeze on television stations shortly after she bought hers. This meant she owned the only television station west of the Mississippi and north of San Francisco.

And people were suddenly crazy for television.

She was definitely in the right place at the right time.

She had the luck and the location.

And she plugged right in to the lunacy that was television.

Pretty soon, even Chamber of Commerce types were admitting that the best businessman in Seattle was a woman.

The Dizzy Fifties

THINGS WERE PROCEEDING at a dizzying pace in Seattle in the 1950s. After fooling around for a quarter of a century, public opinion demanded that the Alaskan Way Viaduct be built. You could get through the city center from the north end in three minutes instead of what sometimes took three hours—and at midnight took ten times the three minutes.

Boeing was fighting the cold war with the Soviet Union for the United States and was providing a lot of jobs in Seattle in the process.

John M. Budd of the Northern Pacific, the son of Jim Hill's right-hand man, had gone crazy and with Robert MacFarlane had taken on the Interstate Commerce Commission and the U.S. Department of Justice in a quixotic effort to regroup the Hill lines that had made Seattle the most important port on the Pacific Coast in the first place.

Didn't they know that was anti-trust, anti-American, anti-government . . . anti-everything?

Merge the Hill lines again?

See you in the Supreme Court first.

And, the Skinner family.

They were the ones who stayed despite the Cotterill-inspired liquor raids.

And what were they doing?

I'm glad you asked that question.

They were helping to invent a thing called the modern container. There were only 3,000 of them in the world in 1959. There are 80,000,000 in use today.

Nikita Khrushchev's revelations about the number of Russians killed by Stalin caused an abrupt turnabout in public opinion over the fact that Seattle was the most strike-ridden city on the Pacific Coast.

Stalin had simply murdered the opposition. In the 1950s the waterfront employers cut the longshoremen in for a piece of the action.

The union members' cut of the savings effected by containers was $8 million in the first five years.

Reorienting Ourselves

And we needed Japan more than ever.

Oh God, how we needed Japan.

Mayor William F. Devin seemed to spend more time there than in the mayor's office.

What we had to get was a Japanese trade fair.

Devin was accompanied to Japan by his friend Sol Levy of the Commission Company. Sol went to Japan to start a Cub Scout movement.

What a lovely pair.

The mayor had instituted an ordinance that required tops on the dancing girls in the city of Seattle.

Sol saw a piece of Japanese merchandise that appealed to him. It was a nutcracker — a nude woman whose legs performed the function that gave the device its name.

Sol began importing these nutcrackers for the Commission Company.

The Port of Seattle was represented in Japan by Colonel Warren Lamport, executive director.

Mayor Devin never took a drink.

Colonel Lamport never turned one down.

John Haydon, brand-new public relations man for the port, went with the colonel to make sure he got to the meetings of the trade delegations. When the colonel was otherwise engaged, John told people what would sell at a Seattle trade fair.

And believe me, they came up with some weird combinations.

The trade fair happened in 1951. It was the first event of its kind in the United States. It gave Seattle a leg up on the competition for the "riches of the Orient."

The exhibit that made John Haydon cringe the most was a string of pearls tossed into the middle of an automobile tire, along with a copy of a General Electric light bulb.

"They simply hadn't got the idea that what we wanted was the best of their culture, not imitations of ours," Haydon said.

When the trade fair opened, the band played the Japanese national anthem for the first time in the United States since the war.

The Japanese in attendance wept . . .

Along with the rest of us.

The trade fair gave us a public relations boost, but it still cost a dollar more to send a ton of Washington apples to Japan through the Port of Seattle than it did through San Francisco or Los Angeles.

The tightwads on the Seattle Port Commission worried more about keeping the rent down on port-owned space for their own businesses than they did about upgrading the facilities to make the port competitive.

Dorothy Bullitt would make sure they had a change of attitude.

Our Dorothy Strikes Again

Meanwhile, she was having such a good time with her Seattle television station that she thought she'd like to buy KGW in Portland. Once again, she had to compete with a rather large establishment. Westinghouse wanted the station, too.

There was a hearing in 1953 before the Federal Communications Commission in Washington, D.C. Dorothy wore her most demur hat and gloves. The Westinghouse lawyers may have relaxed a little when they saw her.

Dorothy noticed at one point that the lawyers had a cart full of documents concerning William Randolph Hearst, who owned 25 percent of KING TV. She realized that Westinghouse was going to use Hearst's unsavory journalistic reputation against her case for acquisition of KGW.

She made a phone call and bought out Hearst's share in KING.

Westinghouse lost one of its major arguments, and Dorothy Bullitt got herself another television station.

The FCC awarded her the Portland franchise largely because of KING TV's fine record of public service and Dorothy's commitment to any community in which she did business.

KING extended its fine record of public service when it produced and aired a program called "Lost Cargo." This was in 1959, and the subject of the program was why Seattle was losing its shirt to the rest of the ports on the Pacific Coast.

Those port commissioners had to sit up and take notice and maybe even do something about the decrepit waterfront.

They had just felt the sting of a Bullitt.

Dorothy Bullitt

What If?

OTHER CITIES HAVE THEIR PSYCHOSES, but Seattle's monomania goes something like this: "Seattle is a one-industry town. What will happen to our economy if?"

It's the jolt of electricity that gets us going in the morning and keeps us running at high speed until we collapse at night. The physical and mental condition of the population keeps the medical profession on its toes, never knowing what we will come up with next, but ready for action, like a boxer entering the ring for the world championship.

Most of the time we don't know what our major industry is, and usually it isn't something that we think it is.

But reality is only what you make it, and if popular opinion makes the wrong thing important, who cares.

It's all public relations.

It started out with Henry Yesler's sawmill.

It was a lousy little mill.

But it had something over all the other sawmills on Puget Sound.

It had steam.

Will the last person to leave turn out the light

That fact that Madam Damnable's whorehouse was the major industry was not something the Puritans prettying the times up for posterity would mention.

When it came to something to worry about, we used Henry's sawmill for a quarter of a century.

For the past fifty years Boeing has been the industry that got ninety-nine percent of the "what ifs."

In 1916 William E. Boeing, a wealthy lumberman's son, founded his company on the banks of the Duwamish River more as a hobby than anything else. He also thought he could make airplanes better than any he had seen other companies turning out.

Within ten years the Boeing Airplane Company had the biggest plant in the United States. Still, it was a quiet operation, with one basic client, the U.S. government.

Philip Johnson was president, and a fellow engineering graduate from the University of Washington, Clair Egtvedt, was vice president.

Boeing got into the airmail business in 1925, submitting a phenomenally low bid to fly the route between Chicago and San Francisco. Johnson and Egtvedt thought they could build a plane that would be cheap enough and efficient enough to make the airmail business profitable. They were right.

Profits soared, and the company expanded.

Pretty soon the Boeing Airplane Company and United Air Lines, formed to handle the transport business, were subsidiaries under the United Aircraft & Transport Company.

Then FDR had his say, and in 1934 Boeing was booted out of the airmail business.

The Air Mail Act of 1934 prohibited any financial link between an airmail transport line and an airplane manufacturer.

United Aircraft & Transport was busted up into three separate companies: United Air Lines, United Aircraft Corporation and the Boeing Airplane Company.

Johnson was banished to Canada. Egtvedt took over at Boeing.

Things looked bad.

Then World War II came along. By 1944, Boeing had 50,000 employees and revenues of $600 million. Its B-17s and B-29s were rolling off the assembly line at the rate of twenty a day. Demand for the planes was so great that even competitors Douglas and Lockheed had to tool up to build the Boeing bombers.

Bill Allen took over and steered the company through its post-war blues. The fifties and sixties were boom years for Boeing.

By 1968, Boeing had 104,000 employees and was gambling its future on the 747 and the SST (supersonic transport).

We know now that only half that gamble paid off.

The Port in the Storm

Fortunately, there were a few other things going on in Seattle in the 1960s.

One very important thing was the new Port Commission, made up of $1-a-year men who already had it made and could think big. They took over in 1960.

John Haydon persuaded them to build container cranes when there were very few containers.

It became cheaper to ship Washington apples to Japan through Washington ports than through the ports in California.

Little things like that.

Then we were also busy making the oil in Alaska something the folks could use to run their motor cars.

And the U.S. government was drilling a $200 million hole on Amchitka to detonate an atom bomb 6,000 feet deep. All the material for that little job flowed through Seattle. (That $200 million was a replay of the Klondike Gold Rush.)

Amchitka is about 100 miles from the Soviet Union. After the bomb went off without throwing any dirt, the Russian spy planes nosing around above the operation waggled their wings in admiration.

In 1962, we helped ourselves to enough money from the U.S. Treasury to pull off the Century 21 Exposition. This affair was more grand and set in the midst of more promise than its 1909 predecessor.

Of all the sacred cows in our history, the Alaska-Yukon-Pacific Exposition is the one we worship most mindlessly.

Hell, if there hadn't been such reverence accorded the AYP, we never would have had the courage to start the Century 21 Exposition.

And then we never would have had the Space Needle as the symbol of our city.

But you can't help wondering what we would have done if we had copied the AYP exactly . . .

Like diverting part of the sewage on the fairgrounds into the fountain drinking water system.

Let's pretend you were one of the people who got typhoid from the water at the AYP.

Let's see, dear reader . . .

Would that have influenced your opinion of the event?

Fortunately, in 1962 we had people like Eddie Carlson to make sure we had a world-class world's fair.

Eddie Carlson had come home from World War II as a lieutenant commander in the U.S. Navy

Before going off to war, he had worked his way up through the ranks for Mr. Thurston, president of an outfit called Western Hotels, which had the leading hotel in places like Wenatchee and Mount Vernon. He had done well enough there that the Rainier Club gave him a job as manager.

His mother was real proud of his advancement to the Rainier Club. This was our most prestigious club. Here Eddie would have a chance to rub elbows with the rich and powerful men in the community.

Some women, too.

They were admitted through a side door but not, of course, permitted in the lobby.

Back from the war, Eddie had all kinds of options. He could go to work for Bill Edris, the lusty owner of the Olympic Hotel, Seattle's *numero uno* hostelry, at a salary of $18,000. He could have his old job back at the Rainier Club and a raise to $12,000. Or he could be Mr. Thurston's assistant and make $6,000.

(Eddie never got over calling S.W. Thurston "Mr. Thurston.")

Let's just say Eddie believes that "the game's the thing. The money is just a system of keeping score."

He took Mr. Thurston's offer, and that's how he came to lead the effort to cancel out the effect of the moral Mr. Cotterill and give Seattle another shot at Queen City status.

A Fair to Remember

Seattle has always had the right man at the right time in the right place to get something done.

Eddie was still there, still willing to gamble, when the time came for the creation of the symbol of our city.

He was appointed chairman of the World's Fair Commission.

He previously had thought winning the Initiative 171 campaign was tough.

Now he was in the big leagues.

It wasn't just those Prohibitionists in the state of Washington who were trying to stop him.

The don'ters in that World's Fair league covered the globe.

Fortunately, Eddie had a country boy with a lot of talent covering his financial bases for him in Washington, D.C. His name was Senator Warren G. Magnuson.

Eddie agreed to take on the fair if Ewen Dingwall would take on the manager's job.

As best I can judge, Dingwall went into a thousand meetings in which he was absolutely flattened. He emerged from each one with a broad smile. His comment, "Great success. Lots of progress made."

Eddie scheduled all the planning sessions for the fair for 7:30 a.m. That was like midday to him. The hour may have discouraged many of the don'ters and insured the opening of the fair.

When the Century 21 Exposition opened, Eddie Carlson was president of the hotel company with which he had cast his lot after World War II. He went on to become chairman of the board. And when Westin and UAL, Inc., merged, he became chairman and chief executive officer of the holding company.

But all this happened after he had made sure Seattle got its symbol . . .

After he pondered how the Seattle fair could capitalize on the launching of the Russian Sputnik . . .

After he went to dinner at the top of a TV tower in Germany and came down with the idea of the Space Needle.

Those Sons of the Profits built the Space Needle on the exposition grounds out of bare steel because they figured they could retrieve $150,000 from the scrap metal after the fair . . .

Whereas if we had covered the stuff with concrete . . .

We would have had nothing . . .

Nada.

Weren't they surprised?

Weren't we all?

The Century 21 Exposition was a huge success. It made money. It made us feel as if we had arrived.

When the Needle went up, so did Seattle's spirit.

Of course, there was still Boeing to worry about.

But we always had to have something . . .

Didn't we?

Something to justify the electrifying question, "What if?"

That's What

WE GOT OUR ANSWER in 1971. I'll be quick about this . . . Like pulling a Band-Aid off . . . It will hurt for only a few seconds, and then we can all breathe again.

In 1971 Bill Allen killed reactivation of the SST project by giving an honest estimate of the cost.

Allen had taken the Boeing Company from 14,000 workers in 1948 to 107,000 in 1970.

His risk-taking had built the company.

His integrity had provided the foundation.

It's a good thing that foundation was solid.

Because by the end of 1971, Boeing had laid off 65,000 workers.

Ouch.

Miner Baker, the leading economist in Seattle, let the world know what trouble we were in: "The overwhelming fact remains that we are losing buckets of blood and it is not within our power to staunch the flow."

Someone more anonymous spent good hard scarce cash for some billboards reading, "Will the last person to leave Seattle please turn out the lights?"

But the lights stayed on.

People didn't leave.

They liked it here.

They were still the bright resourceful people who had been recruited by Boeing.

They stayed and started their own businesses.

What happened as a result of the Boeing layoffs approximates the story of the Mosquito Fleet and the way all that energy and inventiveness triumphed over the faltering giant Northern Pacific in Tacoma.

As she had done a century earlier, Seattle survived.

Boeing's percentage of total employment in the area dropped from eighteen to nine.

Washington was leading the nation in business bankruptcies, but that was just the sign of a lot of activity . . .

A lot of risks being taken.

While the suggestion was being made that the last person in the area should turn out the lights, the Burlington Northern railroad merger was being effected. The system that Jim Hill had put together nearly a century earlier was back in business.

And just in time.

Because the Port of Seattle was ready to take up some of the Boeing slack.

The port was aggressively promoting its new facilities.

It was competitive in what it charged to ship a box of Washington apples.

Hot Potatoes

And French fried potatoes were becoming our fastest growing export.

We grow twice as many Burbank russets to the acre in Washington as they do in Idaho. The Washington State Potato Commission got the state of Idaho sore by running ads saying that Idaho potatoes grow better in Washington.

All those French fries helped make the Port of Seattle one of the most important on the Pacific Coast.

And eighty percent of the goods flowing in and out of the Port of Seattle are carried on the Burlington Northern.

While Miner Baker was worrying about the hemorrhage the Boeing layoffs were causing the city, he should have been paying a bit more attention to what was going on around his desk at Seattle-First National Bank, the largest financial institution in the Northwest.

In a book called Belly Up, Phillip Zweig quoted Seattle-First president William Jenkins as saying, "We are the absorber, not the absorbee."

That was before Bank of America sucked up Seattle-First.

When that happened I asked one of Washington Mutual's former officers what the difference between his bank and Seattle-First was. He replied, rather cattily I thought: "We didn't buy oil wells with other people's money."

Seattle-First was not, of course, the only financial institution to get into trouble during the speculative 1970s.

Moore Fun

We noticed when outsiders bought up our biggest bank. But we didn't respond with anywhere near the outrage that a different set of outsiders met with when they tried to take away the bones that Seattle First had given the city.

Henry Moore's Vertebrae has been gracing the Seafirst Plaza on Fourth Avenue ever since the bank bought the work for $165,000 and installed it there in 1971.

We think of that sculpture as an integral part of Seattle.

"They might as well sell the Space Needle," remarked one indignant resident as he went to view Vertebrae for what he thought was the last time.

That was over an end-of-August weekend in 1986, when the parties involved had planned to crate up the sculpture and cart it down to the Burlington Northern dock for shipment to Japan.

They thought no one would notice.

They were a California bank, a Chicago real estate firm and a Boston art dealer.

They were wrong.

The Seattle bureaucracy has never moved so fast.

The Department of Land Use and Construction slapped a stop-work order on the removal of the sculpture the day it was supposed to go to its new home in Japan.

Someone found a technicality, a $70 demolition permit that they had forgotten to get for their million-dollar deal with a Japanese businessman.

That $70 oversight may have been one of the costliest in Seattle history.

Henry Moore died on August 31, 1986.

The value of Vertebrae was suddenly double what it had been the day before.

But the people of Seattle didn't care about the price.

A lot in Seattle is for sale.

But not our backbone, thank you very much.

Chicago and California had to give in.

Bank of America and JMB Property Management, the Chicago company that had bought the sculpture from Seafirst in 1986 to go with the Seafirst Building, purchased in 1983, ponied up a million bucks each so that the Seattle Art Museum could buy Vertebrae.

The folks at JMB had thought they could make an easy piece of change by selling the sculpture they had bought for $850,000 to Japan for a million. They learned they should stick to the real estate business.

We learned that when we need it, our backbone is there.

This History Is Not Ruthless

S O THAT ABOUT brings us up to date. We're into the second
quarter of our second century now, and nothing much has
changed. We're still what we are because of those rare individu-
als willing to take a chance.

Maybe a few details are different . . .

Like the way we view our history.

For the first century, our past was peopled by saintly types. Then in
1951 Murray Morgan's Skid Road liberated some of those wonder-
fully colorful skeletons from the Seattle family closet. And since that
milestone event, a number of us have had a joyous time writing our
rascals back into our history.

Another difference in detail shows up in the attention we're beginning to pay to the under-utilized, under-recognized half of the population.

Maybe one day soon that historical marker on Second and James will
be amended to credit Louisa Boren with laying the foundations of the
first building in our city.

And there ought to be some way we can publicly acknowledge Lou
Graham's contribution. I hope I've dropped enough clues here to

Tightroping

encourage some broad-minded historian to do the digging necessary to secure Lou's place in the Seattle pantheon.

You can see how attitudes are changing by the time we get to Dorothy Bullitt. Everybody who knows anything about our city knows that she holds a top spot in the tradition that has made us Queen City of the Pacific.

What she did was to put her horse to the highest jump she ever had tried.

And in the process she became Seattle's most powerful woman.

There is one standard that every Seattleite understands.

There is one standard that everyone in the world understands.

Money.

Dorothy Bullitt had a lot of the stuff . . .

Three hundred millions worth.

I don't know how many of the stories about her are apocryphal, but one of my favorites involves the Monorail, which is such a familiar feature of the city. It, of course, takes you from the Westlake Mall to the Space Needle and is considered by many to be our modern umbilical cord.

After the world's fair the Alweg Corporation tried to sell the Monorail to the city of Seattle for several million dollars.

"Tell them to repossess," Dorothy suggested.

Subsequently, there was an item in the Seattle Times noting that the Alweg Corporation was making a generous donation of the Monorail to the city.

The Missing Link

Another woman has an important, some would say controversial, connection with another distinctive transportation feature of our city.

That would be Ruth Neslund, widow of the 81-year-old Puget Sound ship pilot Rolf Neslund, who on the night of June 11, 1978, accidentally rammed the *Antones Chavez* into the Spokane Street bridge.

That is the bridge connecting West Seattle to Seattle.

After Rolf's miscalculation, the bridge remained in its upright position, which it had originally assumed so that the *Antones Chavez* could pass unimpeded beneath.

A number of irate Vashon Islanders missed the 12:30 ferry that night.

The engineering firm that had built the bridge in the first place was asked to estimate the damage and the time it would take for repairs. The estimate was two million dollars and a couple of months.

Then the Seattle spirit descended.

For approximately a century, we had been attempting an adequate hookup with West Seattle, one of our most important communities. By relying on the county or city-run systems, we have never had the quite connection we needed.

After Rolf Neslund's accident, however, we were able to go to the federal government and parlay that two million into two hundred million.

We were able to forge a proper link with West Seattle.

We were also able to free up a huge section of Duwamish riverfront for the city's port facilities when needed.

But in the midst of this windfall, someone is suffering.

That would be Ruth Neslund.

What happened was that the disgrace of his ramming the bridge caused Rolf Neslund to disappear. An Island County prosecutor, with help from the attorney general, convicted Ruth of assisting her husband's departure to regions unknown.

I say that we need to face up to the truth about how important Rolf Neslund was to the city. We need to name the new bridge the Rolf Neslund Memorial Span.

Then we can spring Ruth. No one would want to imprison the widow of a hero with a bridge named after him.

Maybe Ruth is not the best example of what I'm trying to say here about women. But she and I have become great pen pals since she went away to the Purdy Correctional Center. And I've developed a certain sympathy for her slant on things.

I think history in general is richer for admitting the female perspective. And it's not only history that is beginning to catch up on the important role women have played.

The future, too, is encouraging their contributions more and more.

Take Edith Martin, Ph.D.

During World War II, Boeing was noted for its dragon's teeth, that row of fearsome bombers.

Today Boeing stands out because of its Dragon Lady.

"That's Doctor Dragon Lady to you, sir," Edith Martin corrected me the day I met her.

She is a vice president in charge of the Boeing Electronics Company's High Technology Center.

She decides which technologies Boeing will pursue into the next century.

Her job is to take risks.

Edith Martin may not be a familiar name to you now. But she's making a difference to Seattle.

She's the first woman Boeing has given the vice presidential designation.

She stands for a whole generation of women getting recognition for the risks they take.

It's hard not to personalize this whole subject when so many women have played such an important role in my life, like the one who has gone through thick and thin with me for the last thirty-seven years.

Or the one who said, "The reader doesn't give a shit how hard it was for you to get the material for this book."

Or the one who has been my right-hand associate for nearly half a century.

Or MJ, who helped save Seattle's Underground and said of one of my obstacles, "He's trying to make his job small enough for him to encompass."

Back to the Beginning

And that brings me to another one of my favorite subjects . . .

Pioneer Square.

After World War II was over and the white flight to suburbia had begun, City Engineer Charlie Wartelle looked at Pioneer Square and wailed, "We spent a million dollars a square block to make this the finest city center on earth and now they are throwing it away . . ."

Architect Vic Steinbrueck did an article on how that fine old city center could be saved.

And my wife Shirley, who thinks I can do anything she makes up her mind to, said, "Why don't you get Pioneer Square restored?"

Norton Clapp doesn't even remember this, but he primed the pump with the only thing that would work . . .

That universal standard again . . .

Money.

At first we got the window washers' union to agree to wash all the windows in what then was known as the more colorful Skid Road.

And the carpenters' union to agree to make window boxes.

And a lumber yard to provide the lumber.

And the Women's Garden Clubs to plant and maintain flowers in the window boxes.

The building owners had a meeting . . .

And read a prepared statement turning down the plan.

Those were the days when the engineers were running rampant, and the sinking ship garage in the middle of Pioneer Square became its present awful reality.

And that's when we discovered that Seattle had an Underground where the city's beginnings were moldering away beneath the present-day streets.

In 1964 we began a novelty called the Underground Tour.

And the Central Association began its annual effort to get the Underground replaced with skyscrapers . . .

And the wives of the men in the Central Association attended the same city council meetings opposing them.

In San Francisco, Mayor Dorm Braman was saying: "Show me what you're going to replace these old building with or I won't let you tear them down."

The mayor of Sacramento failed to do that, and Interstate 5 plowed through that city's underground, destroying it.

Finally, architect Ralph Anderson swallowed his gum and restored a building at First and Jackson.

The center of Pioneer Square was three blocks away.

The Sons of the Profits who sensed that restoration was coming wanted an arm and a leg for their buildings.

By the time Wes Uhlman was elected mayor, we had collected 30,000 signatures on a petition to restore the city's birthplace.

Wes alerted restoration advocates that the Central Association was sending one man for each city council member to San Francisco.

The Central Association was allegedly making the trip to study Bay Area Rapid Transit.

In reality, they were taking a last stab at making Pioneer Square safe for skyscrapers.

But restoration activist Gigi Platt met the whole group at the San Francisco airport and kidnapped the Seattle City Council out from under the noses of the Central Association representatives and showed the council members what restoration looked like.

At midnight on the steps of the Saint Francis Hotel, the members of the city council shook Gigi's hand and swore, "The Pioneer Square/

Skid Road Ordinance will pass."

We were saved by the "belle."

Later, when the Kingdome threatened to destroy what had been so recently saved, I took my worries to Wes. And the mayor said: "Fear not. We will provide the city engineer with givens: Given lowered lighting . . . Given trees planted in the center of First Avenue South . . . Given a pedestrian mall on Occidental Avenue South . . . How will you get traffic from the stadium to the retail shopping center around Frederick's and the Bon?"

The city engineer had no choice but to route traffic around Pioneer Square.

In Sacramento, citizens had to spend more than a hundred million bucks of public money to make a public park of their old town.

So if you can find your way there through the concrete spaghetti of Interstate 5, you can see a forever drain of public funds.

Whereas in Pioneer Square, private funds did the restoration work. Between 1980 and 1985, $199,000,000 in private funds were applied to Pioneer Square's "dead" buildings . . .

Putting them back on the tax rolls.

And the Space Needle . . .

It's paying taxes while all the buildings around it in Seattle Center are crying for a handout.

Pioneer Square is one of half a dozen neighborhoods that give Seattle character and individuality.

Our birthplace reborn.

A Question of Paternity

Another one of our unique and colorful neighborhoods is the Pike Place Market area.

On Friday, February 15, 1985, the Seattle Post-Intelligencer carried a headline reading: "Pike Market's 'father' Victor Steinbrueck dies."

Vic got the title because virtually single-handedly he stood up against the Seattle Establishment and won the fight to preserve and restore the market.

There were the forces who wanted to "high rise" the market, leaving only a token of the past. They called themselves the Committee to Save the Market.

Vic headed an organization called the Friends of the Market.

The voters had to figure out which one really proposed to preserve the market. They had a tough time with the names of the two organizations.

But they did know where Vic stood.

So they voted for Vic . . .

Two to one.

But was he really father of the market?

When Vic and I were fellow students at Franklin High School, a place that recently won a restoration battle of its own, we both believed that Joe Desimone was the father of the Pike Place Market.

Since our names were close together in the alphabet, we often had adjoining desks in the late 1920s at Franklin. We shared a few other things that are not mentionable here, including comments like, "when I kick the bucket . . ."

And one of the things we would definitely have questioned was the title Vic got in his obituary.

We knew that Joe was the Pike Place progenitor.

God knows how, but Joe acquired forty bucks as a young man growing up on the Isle of Rhodes. He stowed away on a ship that landed at Ellis Island, where he persuaded an immigration official to look the other way while he sneaked into the United States.

Wait a minute . . .

God was not the only one who knew about Joe's knack for getting money.

The Seattle City Council must have known.

It gave him the key to the treasury at Pike Place Market, or at least that's what some of his compatriots said. And the way they said it was, "God didn't have nothin' to do with it."

Joe became the market's first millionaire. And like a lot of other people who became millionaires, he did not necessarily subscribe to the Marquis of Queensbury rules. And he made money on rich bottomland before the Kent Valley was Boeingized.

Now it's costing us millions of dollars to buy up that bottomland and other fertile farmlands that help make up our recently discovered "environment."

But it's only money, and it's worth it.

And while the farmers at the Pike Place Market are fewer than the 600 who once managed to beat out the middleman for a while, the place is still called the cradle of small business in Seattle.

It is here and at a low rental that is partially government subsidized that about 150 people with an idea for a new business can try it out on the public annually . . .

Free enterprise with a governmental assist.

That's what Vic was the father of.

He also shared paternity of the Space Needle.

I know I mentioned it at the beginning of this book.

But I think a man's dying wish is a pretty serious thing.

It was two days before he died that Vic called me from his hospital bed in Seattle to say, "Don't you dare let those bastards give John Graham credit for the design of the Space Needle."

Okay, Vic.

It's your Needle whose eye I've been squinting through for my look at Seattle's history.

Thanks for the view.

Acknowledgments, Sources, Bibliography

Many people assisted Bill Speidel in the research of this book. Since Bill kept so much information in his own "personal computer" we have most probably left out many important people who significantly added to the research of this book; for that please accept our apologies.

Jonelle Simonian for her endless research, especially into the estate of Lou Graham. Tom Pratt and Nelson Phillips for their help in teaching Bill how to use his first computer.

Joshua Green and Henry Broderick for their aural history on Jacob Furth and Lou Graham, with the understanding that the material not be used until after their deaths.

Edith Martin for her information on Boeing Electronics and how she became the first woman VP at Boeing.

Thanks to Vashon Library for all of their work, with a special thanks to Marie Metzker and Shirley Porro for their patience.

George and Pat Roberts for their fast and accurate computer work and for their superb proofreading.

Emmett Watson for his foreword.

Thanks should go to Jim Ellis, Fred Baker, Jim Ryan and I am sure countless others whom Bill interviewed but did not have a chance to write about. Bill saw these people, and others, as ones who have shaped our "recent history."

Others who deserve special mention are Candace Lein-Hayes and Mike Saunders from the Washington State and King County Archives, who verified so many facts for Bill. Yvonne Prater for her excellent knowledge of Snoqualmie Pass. Bob Wing from Puget Power for his information regarding Jacob Furth and the beginning of the Seattle Electric Light Company. Patsy Collins and Dorothy Bullitt for their invaluable information regarding Seattle's past and KING Television.

Bob Crandall, of Winthrop, Washington, for his invaluable information on Saltwater Bill, Jacob Furth and "The run on the bank."

BOOKS

BAGLEY, Clarence B.; *History of Seattle From the Earliest Settlement to the Present Time.* 3 vols. Chicago, S.J. Clarke, 1916. *History of King County.* 3 vols. Chicago, S.J. Clarke, 1929.

BARTO, H. E. and BULLARD, Catherine; *History of the State of Washington.* Heath Publishing, 1924.

BEATON, Welford; *The City That Made Itself.* Seattle, Terminal Publishing Co., 1914.

BRODERICK, Henry; *The H.B. Story and Seattle's Yesterdays.* Seattle, Frank McCaffrey, 1969.

BURKE, Padriac; *A History of the Port of Seattle.* Seattle, University of Washington, 1976.

CLARK, Norman H.; *The Dry Years: Prohibition and Social Change in Washington.* Seattle, University of Washington Press, 1965.

DENNY, Arthur Armstrong; *Pioneer Days on Puget Sound.* Seattle, Ye Galleon Press Reproductions.

DENNY, Emily Inez; *Blazing the Way.* Seattle, Historical Society of Seattle, 1909.

DRYDEN, Cecil; *History of Washington.* Portland, Binfords & Mort, 1968.

GATES, Charles M.; *The First Century at the University of Washington.* Seattle, University of Washington, 1961.

GRANT, Frederic James; *History of Seattle.* New York, American Publishing and Engraving Co., 1891.

HANFORD, C. H.; *Seattle and Environs.* Chicago and Seattle, Pioneer Historical Publishing Company, 1924.

HILL, James J.; *Highways of Progress.* New York, Doubleday Page & Co, 1910.

HINES, Neal O.; *Denny's Knoll.* Seattle and London, University of Washington Press, 1980.

JOHNSON, Edwin F.; *Railroad to the Pacific.* Seattle, Ye Galleon Press Reproductions, 1981.

JONES, Nard; *Seattle.* New York, Doubleday & Co., New York, 1972.

MANSFIELD, Harold; *Vision, A Saga of the Sky.* New York, Duell, Sloan & Pearce, 1956.

MARTIN, Albro; *James J. Hill and the Opening of the Northwest.* New York, Oxford University Press, 1976.

MCWILLIAMS, Mary; *Seattle Water Department History 1854-1954.* Seattle, Publisher, City of Seattle, 1955.

MORGAN, Murray Cromwell; *Skid Road.* Seattle, University of Washington Press, 1960.

NESBIT, Robert C.; *He Built Seattle, A Biography of Judge Thomas Burke.* Seattle, University of Washington Press, 1961.

NEWELL, Gordon; *The Green Years.* Seattle.

PRATER, Yvonne; *Snoqualmie Pass.* Seattle, The Mountaineers, 1981.

PROSCH, Thomas Wickham; *David S. Maynard and Catherine T. Maynard.* Seattle, Lowman & Hanford, 1906.

SALES, Roger; *Seattle, Past to Present.* Seattle, University of Washington Press, 1976.

SCATES, Shelby; *Firstbank . . . The Story of Seattle-First National Bank.* Seattle, Publisher, Sea1st Bank, 1970.

TAYLOR, Frank J.; *High Horizons.* McGraw-Hill, 1955.

WATT, Mrs. Roberta (Frye); *The Story of Seattle; Four Wagons West.* Portland, Binfords & Mort, 1931.

WING, Robert C., Editor; *A Century of Service, The Puget Sound Story.* Bellevue, Publisher, Puget Sound Power & Light, 1987.

GOVERNMENT SOURCES

King County Library, Vashon Branch; San Francisco Health Department; Seattle Health Department; Seattle Water Department; State Archives, Olympia; Washington State Library, Olympia; Port of Seattle; N.W. Collection Library at the University of Washington.

CONTEMPORARY NEWSPAPERS AND PERIODICALS

Argus, Northwest Magazine; Seattle Post-Intelligencer/Seattle Times; The Weekly; Port of Seattle *Tradelines.*

Index